Library of Congress Cataloging-in-Publication Data
Hayward, Linda. The Sesame Street dictionary.
SUMMARY: A dictionary of the vocabulary of very young children, presenting for each word a definition,
a sentence using the word, and an illustration of the sentence featuring Sesame Street characters.
1. Picture dictionaries, English—Juvenile literature. [1. Picture dictionaries]
I. Mathieu, Joseph. II. Sesame Street. III. Sesame Workshop. IV. Title.
PE1629.H3 423 80-11644
ISBN-10: 0-375-82810-9
ISBN-13: 978-0-375-82810-2

MANUFACTURED IN SINGAPORE 11 10 9 8 7 6 5

www.sesamestreetbooks.com
www.randomhouse.com/kids
www.sesamestreet.com

The Sesame Street Dictionary

By Linda Hayward

Illustrated by Joe Mathieu

Random House New York

Since its debut in 1969, the *Sesame Street* television show has made—and still makes—learning an enjoyable and natural part of daily life for millions of children. *The Sesame Street Dictionary* fosters the same important educational goals. More than a standard beginner's dictionary, its many unique features make it a book with which a child can *grow* from age three to age eight. It has been carefully designed to be used in three stages:

- as a word book and vocabulary builder,
- as a reading-readiness storybook,
- as a first dictionary.

A primary goal of *The Sesame Street Dictionary* is to make using a dictionary an enjoyable as well as a rewarding experience. The exciting and humorous visual presentation invites the exploration of words and helps establish at an early age a positive attitude toward using dictionaries. Long before a child is old enough to read, he or she can *see* that this dictionary is fun. At the same time, *The Sesame Street Dictionary* provides accurate, complete, and easily understood information. More than 1,300 words are defined, illustrated, and used in context in one or more sample sentences.

The definitions are short, straightforward, and unusually clear and accurate. The vocabulary is structured for beginning readers. In all cases the definitions reflect the primary meaning of the word in terms of a child's world.

The dictionary concentrates on words that appear frequently in beginning reading books and in a young child's everyday world. Other words, such as *rocket, dinosaur,* and *skeleton,* were chosen because they fascinate children.

The lively, colorful illustrations reinforce and in many cases expand the definition of the word. For example, the verb *blow* is illustrated with four pictures in which a Muppet first blows *on* a trombone, then blows *up* a balloon, blows *away* bubbles, and finally blows *out* a birthday candle. This comic-strip-style flexibility gives the dictionary an exciting storybook appearance.

Children using this dictionary will quickly become familiar with the conventions used throughout. Amazing Mumford, the magician, pulls homonyms out of his hat, such as *bat* and *bat,* one being a baseball bat and the other a flying bat. A twiddlebug signals an exception or additional meaning. For example, one twiddlebug points out after the word *bean* that a jelly*bean* is only candy shaped like a *bean.* Each section closes with a humorous complaint from Oscar the Grouch. After the *R* section he asks, "How can you have a dictionary without words like *rude* and *rubbish* and *rotten*?" A head word at the top of each page helps the child practice the use of alphabetization and prepares him or her for graduating into the longer, intermediate-grade dictionaries.

Games, riddles, and jokes are another unique feature of this book. These activities are used not only to reinforce word meanings but also to present educational concepts such as naming the parts of the body, counting, sorting objects by their characteristics, measuring, and relationships.

We hope that you use this dictionary to help make learning new words an incredible adventure that lasts for a lifetime.

—The Sesame Workshop Education and Research Department

a   A is a word that means one.

Bert is reaching for **a** book.

able   When you are able to do something, you can do it.

Bert is **able** to reach the book. Ernie is not **able** to reach that high.

about   About means on the subject of.

> I wonder what this dictionary says **about** pigeons.

A dictionary is a book **about** words.

about   About can also mean a little more or a little less or almost.

> There are **about** thirteen hundred words in this dictionary.

above   When you are above something, you are higher than it is.

> Hello, everybod-ee! I, Grover, am flying my little airplane **above** the trees.

> Uh-oh! Now I am *not* **above** the trees.

accident   An accident is something that happens by mistake.

> Oops! Your old pal Grover had a little **accident**.

across   When you go across something, you move from one side to the other side.

act   When you act, you pretend to be someone or something else.

actor   An actor is someone who acts.

Ernie and Bert are **actors.** They are acting in a play. The audience is watching them.

add   When you add to something, you make it bigger.

add   When you add numbers or things, you find out how many there are all together.

address   Your address is where you live.

Ernie and Bert live at 123 Sesame Street. 123 Sesame Street is their **address.**

adult   An adult is someone who has grown up.

adventure   An adventure is something exciting that happens to someone.

afraid   When you feel afraid, you are scared or frightened.

Grover is **afraid** of the dark.

after   After means later than.

afternoon   Afternoon is the time of the day that comes between morning and night.

again   When you do something again, you do it one more time.

against   Against means upon or touching.

against   Against can also mean on opposite sides.

The Red Monster team is playing **against** the Blue Monster team.

age   Your age is how old you are.

The Busby twins are the same **age.**

agree   When people agree, they think the same way or want the same things.

The Busby twins **agree** about striped shirts.

ahead   When you are ahead, you are in front.

The tortoise and the hare are having a race. The hare is **ahead.**

air   Air is what you breathe. Air is all around you. It is what you feel when the wind blows.

airplane   An airplane is something that you ride in. An airplane has wings and can move through the sky.

airport   An airport is a place where airplanes take off and land.

Grover is landing his **airplane** at the **airport**.

alarm   An alarm is a buzzer or a bell that wakes you or warns you.

The **alarm** on Big Bird's clock wakes him up.

The fire **alarm** warns the fire fighters that there is a fire.

alive   Things that are alive need food and water.

Plants are **alive**.

Animals are **alive**.

People are **alive**.

Rocks are not **alive**.

alike   When things are alike, they are the same.

The Busby twins look **alike**.

all All means everything with nothing left over.

Gee, Bert, I don't know. I guess you have **all** the luck.

Ernie, why am I carrying **all** the groceries?

alligator An alligator is an animal with lots of teeth and a long tail.

Hi! My name is Prairie Dawn. I wonder why most people are afraid of **alligators.**

Oh!

allow When you allow people to do something, you let them do it.

It has come to my attention that some of you are smiling. Well, smiling is not **allowed.** If you promise not to smile, I will **allow** you to read this dictionary.

almost Almost means nearly.

The cookies are **almost** gone.

alone When you are alone, no one is with you.

Hello again! Remember me? I am the Count and I love to count things. When I am **alone,** I count myself. 1…one Count!

along When you go along something, you move from one end toward the other end.

Sherlock Hemlock is walking **along** Sesame Street.

along Along can also mean together with.

Ernie took Rubber Duckie **along** with him.

aloud   Aloud means loud enough to be heard, not in a whisper.

Big Bird likes to read **aloud.**

ABCDEFG...
HIJKLMNOP...
QRS...TUV...
WXYZ.

ALPHABET BOOK

alphabet   The alphabet is all the letters from A to Z.

I, Sherlock Hemlock, the world's greatest detective, have discovered the world's longest word.

Oh, Sherlock! That's not a word. It's the **alphabet.**

Another way of saying **alphabet** is ABCs.

already   Already means before now.

The Count is going to bed. He has **already** brushed his teeth.

also   Also means too.

abcdefghijklmno
pqrstuvwxyz

Hi! I'm Roosevelt Franklin. I know my letters from A to Z. I **also** know my numbers from 1 to 20.

1 2 3 4 5 6 7 8 9 10
11 12 13 14 15 16 17 18 19 20

always   Always means all the time or every time.

Cookie Monster has a big appetite. He is **always** hungry.

Ernie **always** has Rubber Duckie with him when he takes a bath.

am Do you want to play WHO **AM** I?

among Among means in with or in the middle of.

Bert likes to walk **among** the pigeons.

among Among can also mean with some for each.

amount Amount means how much or how many.

an An means one.

Grover is eating **an** apple.

and And means together with or also.

angry When you get mad, you feel angry.

Ernie, please pick up these toys right away! This place is a mess!

Bert is **angry.**

animal An animal is any living thing that is not a plant. An animal can move from one place to another by itself. Most plants cannot.

Farmer Grover is feeding the **animals** on his farm.

another Another means one more.

I am picking a flower.

I am picking **another** flower. Now I have two flowers.

answer An answer is what you say to a question.

How much is one plus one?

The **answer** is two.

answer When you answer, you say something back.

Grover!

Yes, Mommy! I am coming!

When Grover's mother calls, Grover always **answers.**

ant An ant is a small, crawling insect.

Look! The **ants** are taking my picnic lunch! Am I angry? No, I am happy. Now I can count them. 1, 2, 3, 4, 5… five wonderful **ants**!

any Any means one or some.

We grouches don't like **any**body or **any**one or **any**thing. Turn the page so I will not have to look at you **any**more.

apartment An apartment is a place to live in. There are many apartments in an apartment building.

Bert is playing the accordion in his **apartment**.

appear When something appears, you can see it.

I, the Amazing Mumford, will wave my magic wand and a rabbit will **appear**.

A LA PEANUT BUTTER SANDWICHES!

Now where is that rabbit?

apple An apple is a fruit that grows on an apple tree.

Here is my favorite thing that begins with A—**apple**.

And here is *my* favorite thing that begins with A—**apple** core.

are Big Bird and Snuffle-upagus **are** best friends.

You **are** my best friend, Mr. Snuffle-upagus.

You **are** *my* best friend, Bird.

arm Your arm is the part of your body between your shoulder and your hand. Look up the word body.

around Around means in a circle.

Marshal Grover has a belt **around** his waist.

I have turned **around**. You cannot see my face.

artist An artist is someone who makes or does special things.

Some **artists** make pictures.

Some **artists** make statues.

Some **artists** dance.

Some **artists** play musical instruments.

as As means equal to.

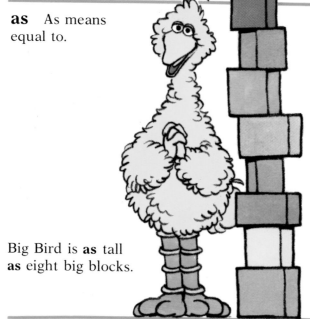

Big Bird is **as** tall **as** eight big blocks.

ask You ask a question when you want to find out the answer.

A detective has to **ask** many questions.

Who? What? Where? When? How? Why?

asleep When you are asleep, you are not awake.

I wonder if Bert is **asleep**.... Oh, Bert. Are you **asleep**?

He doesn't hear me. I'll have to speak louder. HEY, BERT! ARE YOU **ASLEEP**?

No, Ernie. You woke me up. I *was* **asleep**. Now I am awake.

astronaut An astronaut is someone who travels in a spaceship.

One small step for Grover Monster— one giant step for Monsterkind!

Grover the **astronaut** is on the moon.

at At tells when or where.

At night Little Bird likes to stay **at** home.

attention When you pay attention, you look and listen.

Herry Monster is not paying **attention**. He is bumping into everything.

aunt Your aunt is the sister of your mother or father.

Aunt Sally is my mother's sister. Aunt Elma is my father's sister.

author An author is someone who writes stories, poems, or plays.

Big Bird is the **author** of *Birds of a Feather*.

autumn Autumn is the name of a season. Autumn comes after summer. Another name for autumn is fall.

It must be **autumn**. The leaves are turning red and yellow.

awake When you are awake, you are not sleeping.

Bert is still **awake**.

away Away means somewhere else.

At last! This is the end of the A words. Now you can go **away** and leave me alone.

Bb

A B C D E F G H I J K L M N O P Q R S T U V W X Y Z

baby   A baby is a very young child.

What do monsters have that nobody else has?

Baby monsters!

back   Your back is the part of your body opposite your chest and between your neck and your hips. Look up the word body.

Prairie Dawn is hiking. She has a pack on her **back**.

back   The back is also the part of a thing that is behind the front.

Grover's airplane has a propeller in front and a tail in **back**.

bad   When something is bad, it is not good.

This is a **bad** day for a picnic.

When you feel bad, you don't feel good.

Bert has caught a cold. He feels **bad**.

Ernie is sorry that Bert is sick. Ernie feels **bad**.

bag A bag is a kind of container. You can put things in a bag.

bake When you bake something, you cook it in an oven.

baker A baker is someone who bakes.

bakery A bakery is the place where a baker bakes. A bakery is also a store where you can buy the things the baker bakes.

Everybody comes to Cookie's **bakery** to buy the cookies Cookie the **baker bakes.**

ball A ball is something to play with. Most balls are round.

balloon A balloon is a bag made of rubber. It can be filled with air or another kind of gas.

Prairie Dawn is blowing up a **balloon.**

banana A banana is a fruit that grows on banana trees.

band   A band is a group of people playing musical instruments together.

band   A band is also a strip of material that goes around something.

bank   A bank is a place or thing to keep money in.

bank   A bank is also the high ground along the side of a river.

barber   A barber is someone who cuts your hair.

Farley went to the **barber**shop. The **barber** cut Farley's hair.

bark   A bark is a sound that a dog makes.

Barkley the dog can **bark** very loudly. The tree **bark** cannot.

bark   Bark is also the outside covering of a tree.

barn   A barn is a building on a farm where the farmer keeps cows, horses, hay, and grain.

Farmer Grover is going to his **barn** to milk his cows.

basket   A basket is a kind of container. You can put things in a basket.

Here is my favorite **basket**— a picnic **basket** filled with apples and bananas and peanut butter sandwiches.

Here is *my* favorite **basket**— a waste**basket**. Just look at all this wonderful crumpled-up paper!

bat   A bat is a small, furry animal that flies.

bat   A bat is also a wooden stick. You can hit a ball with a bat.

I, the Amazing Mumford, will now pull from this perfectly empty hat two different things with the same name—

A LA PEANUT BUTTER SANDWICHES!

A baseball **bat** and a flying **bat**.

bath When you take a bath, you wash all over.

bathtub A bathtub is a thing in which you take a bath.

Ernie and Rubber Duckie are taking a **bath** in the **bathtub.**

be To be is to live or exist.

I will plant these seeds, and soon there will **be** carrots growing here.

be Sometimes we use the word be to tell someone how to act.

Be careful not to step on my seeds!

beach A beach is the sandy or pebbly land next to an ocean, a lake, or a river.

Ernie and Bert are at the **beach.**

bean A bean is a vegetable.

Here are some **beans.** They are all delicious.

string bean

kidney bean

lima bean

A jelly**bean** is not a vegetable. It is a piece of candy shaped like a **bean.**

jellybean

bear A bear is a big, furry animal.

Once upon a time there were three **bears**—

beautiful When something you see or hear pleases you very much, you say it is beautiful.

because Because is a word that tells why.

bed A bed is a place to sleep.

bee A bee is a flying insect that buzzes. Some bees sting.

before Before is a word that means earlier than.

This is the chair **before** Herry Monster sat in it.

This is the chair after Herry Monster sat in it.

begin When you begin, you start.

beginning The beginning is the start of something.

Prairie Dawn always gets excited at the **beginning** of her favorite TV show.

behind When you are behind something, you are in back of it.

Farley is sitting **behind** Prairie Dawn. He wishes he were in front of her.

believe When you believe something, you think it is true.

Mr. Snuffle-upagus is real. But nobody **believes** me.

I **believe** you, Bird.

belong When something belongs to you, you own it.

Rubber Duckie **belongs** to Ernie.

belong When something belongs, it is in the right place.

Hey, Bert. Three of these things **belong** together. One of these things is not the same.

That's right, Ernie. That sock is a piece of clothing. The other things are toys. They **belong** in your toy box! What are they doing in my laundry basket?

bell A bell is something that rings.

Roosevelt Franklin is ringing his bicycle **bell.**

Cookie Monster is ringing a door**bell.**

below

When you are below something, you are lower than it is.

I, Grover, am flying my little airplane **below** the clouds. Hello, up there, little cloud!

beside

When you are beside something, you are next to it.

Herry Monster is standing **beside** the Busby twins.

between

When you are between two things, you are in the space that separates them.

Herry Monster is standing **between** the Busby twins.

bicycle

A bicycle is a machine that people ride. It has two wheels, handlebars, and pedals to make the wheels go around.

Grover likes to ride his **bicycle.**

Another name for a **bicycle** is bike.

big

Something big needs more room than something little. It is large, not small.

Big Bird needs a **big** nest.

Little Bird needs a little nest.

bird

A bird is an animal with feathers and a beak. Most birds can fly.

Big **Bird**'s feathers are yellow.

birthday   Your birthday is the day of the year when you were born.

bite   When you take a bite of something, you break off a piece with your teeth.

block   A block is a building toy.

block   A block is also a place for buildings in a town or city. Your block is your street from one corner to the other.

blood   Blood is the red liquid that is pumped to all parts of your body by your heart. Blood flows through tubes called veins and arteries.

blow   When you blow, air comes out of your mouth.

Here is something to **blow** on.

Here is something to **blow** up.

Here is something to **blow** away.

Here is something to **blow** out.

board   A board is a flat piece of wood.

Bert has some **boards.**
He is going to build a birdhouse.

NAILS

boat   A boat is something that floats in the water and can carry people and things.

Some **boats** have sails.

Some **boats** have engines.

Some **boats** have oars.

Some **boats** have leaks.

body   Your body is all of you, from the top of your head to the tips of your toes.

bones A bone is a part of your body. Your bones are hard. Look up the word skeleton.

Here is a picture of the **bones** inside a body.

boot A boot is a shoe that covers the ankle.

Ernie is wearing red rain **boots** over his shoes.

Rodeo Rosie is wearing cowgirl **boots** instead of shoes.

born When a baby has grown big enough to be outside its mother's body, it is ready to be born.

This calf was just **born**.

book A book has sheets of paper between two covers. Most books have words. Some books have pictures.

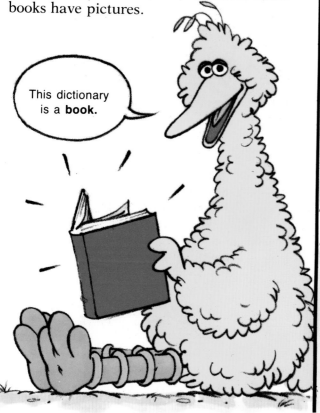

This dictionary is a **book**.

both Both means two together.

Both Biff and Sully are eating lunch.

bottle A bottle is a kind of container, usually made of glass or plastic. A bottle can hold something that you pour.

Sully, pass me that **bottle** of Figgy Fizz, please.

bottom The bottom is the place farthest from the top.

Hey, Bert, old buddy, can I look at one of your bottle caps?

Sure, Ernie.

What did you do that for, Ernie?

I wanted to see the one on the **bottom.**

bow A bow is a fancy knot. When you tie a bow, you make a knot with loops.

bow A bow is also a special kind of stick. It is used to play many stringed instruments.

I, the Amazing Mumford, will now pull from this perfectly empty hat two different things with the same name.

A LA PEANUT BUTTER SANDWICHES!

One beautiful ribbon **bow** and one violin **bow**!

bowl A bowl is a deep, round dish.

What kind of cereal does a ghost put in his cereal **bowl**?

Ghost Toasties!

box A box is a kind of container. You can put things in a box.

Gee, Bert, I didn't know oatmeal came in so many different kinds of **boxes.**

boy A boy is a child who will grow up to be a man.

I am a **boy.** My father is a man. When I grow up, I will be a man, too.

bread Bread is something to eat. It is made from flour and baked in an oven.

Three of these things belong together. One of these things is not the same.

*The clock does not belong. You cannot eat a clock. But you can eat loaves of **bread.***

white bread

French bread

rye bread

clock

break When something breaks, it falls to pieces or stops working.

*Oops! I did not mean to **break** the vase.*

*Ernie, stop playing with the television set or you'll **break** it. Then I won't be able to watch the Pigeon News.*

breakfast Breakfast is the meal that you eat in the morning.

Bert has oatmeal for **breakfast** every day.

bridge A bridge is something that is built across water, roads, or deep valleys. People, cars, and other things can cross over a bridge.

The Count is driving his bat car over the **bridge.**

bring When you bring something, you have it with you when you come.

*Big Bird, you didn't have to **bring** me a present.*

*I **brought** you a new vase.*

broom   A broom is a special kind of brush on the end of a long stick. It is used to sweep up dirt and trash.

Uh-oh! Herry Monster broke the new vase. Big Bird is using a **broom** to sweep up the pieces.

brother   If your mother and father have another child who is a boy, he is your brother.

He is my **brother.**

She is my sister.

brush   A brush is a tool made of bristles fastened to a handle.

Biff wants to paint the hallway. He has a can of paint. Which **brush** is better for Biff?

paint brush

tooth brush

PAINT

Sully wants to clean his teeth. He has some toothpaste. Which **brush** is better for Sully?

build   When you build, you put pieces together to make something.

Bert is going to **build** a birdhouse.

NAILS

Bert is **building** the birdhouse.

building   A building is a place with walls and a roof.

Here is the **building** that Bert built. It is for the birds.

bump When you bump into something, you hit it with your body— usually by mistake.

bump A bump is a lump.

Watch out, Bert! You will **bump** your head.

Bert **bumped** into the birdhouse.

Now Bert has a **bump** on his head.

burn When something catches on fire, it burns. It gives out light and heat.

My candle has started to **burn.** Now I can see to count my pictures. But first, let me count my candle. 1... one candle!

Some things turn to ashes when they **burn.**

bus A bus is something that you ride in. It has lots of seats. A bus can carry many people from place to place.

SESAME STREET

Here comes the **bus**!

READ BOOKS

BUS STOP

Five people are waiting at the **bus** stop.

busy   When you are busy, you have lots to do.

The bird watcher is **busy** watching birds.

The builder is **busy** building a building.

The bus driver is **busy** driving a bus.

The bricklayer is **busy** laying bricks.

but   But means except.

Everyone is busy **but** Big Bird.

I feel like reading, **but** I don't have a book.

butcher   A butcher is someone who cuts and sells meat for people to cook.

Herry Monster went to the **butcher** shop. He bought some meat from the **butcher**.

butterfly   A butterfly is an insect with a thin body and four wings.

Catching a **butterfly** is not easy.

button A button is small and flat and usually round. Some buttons hold clothes together. Some buttons make things work.

> Hey, Ernie, look at all the different **buttons** in my **button** collection.

> Gee, Bert, you are missing the best **button** of all.

> Which one is that?

> The belly**button**. Heh! Heh!

Grover the elevator operator is pushing the **button** for the tenth floor.

> Going up?

buy When you buy something, you pay for it. After you buy something, it belongs to you.

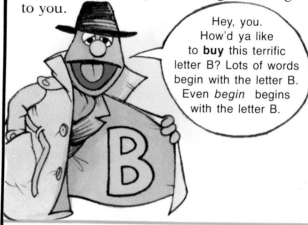

> Hey, you. How'd ya like to **buy** this terrific letter B? Lots of words begin with the letter B. Even *begin* begins with the letter B.

by By means near or beside.

Oscar's garbage can is the one **by** the steps.

GO AWAY!

by If something was done by you, you did it.

> I painted this picture all **by** myself.

BY Big Bird

> These are supposed to be the B words, but I can't even find some of my favorite words that begin with B—words like bellyache, bothersome, blecch, and BEAT IT!

C c

A B C D E F G H I J K L M N O P Q R S T U V W X Y Z

cake   A cake is something sweet to eat. It is usually made with flour, eggs, butter, sugar, and other things.

> Happy birthday, Grover! Me bake **cake** for you.

> Thank you, Cookie Monster!

calendar   A calendar tells you what day it is. It shows the months, weeks, and days of the year. There are seven days in a week and twelve months in a year.

The days of the week are Sunday, Monday, Tuesday, Wednesday, Thursday, Friday, and Saturday.

The months of the year are January, February, March, April, May, June, July, August, September, October, November, and December.

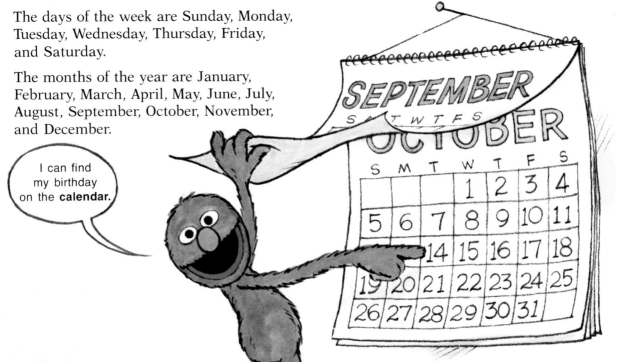

> I can find my birthday on the **calendar.**

call When you call someone, you use a loud voice.

ERNIE!

You don't have to **call** me, Bert. I'm right here.

call When you call on a telephone, you use a telephone to speak to someone.

Hello, operator? I want to **call** my friend Mr. Snuffle-upagus.

Mr. Who?

can A can is a kind of container, usually made of metal. It is used to hold things.

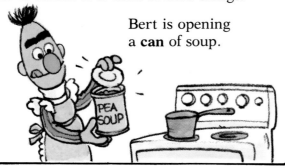

Bert is opening a **can** of soup.

PEA SOUP

can When you can do something, it is possible for you to do it. You are able to do it.

Big Bird **can** reach the shelf.

Little Bird **can**not.

cap A cap is a kind of lid. It covers the top of something else.

Ernie just took the **cap** off a bottle of Figgy Fizz.

Ernie, save that bottle **cap**! I need it for my collection.

cap A cap is also something to wear on your head.

Bert is wearing a shower **cap.**

cape A cape is a coat without sleeves.

Super Grover wears a pink **cape.**

car   A car is something that you ride in.

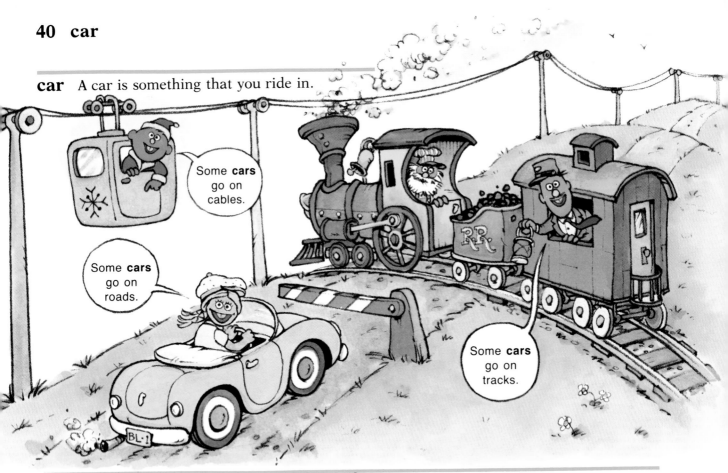

Some **cars** go on cables.

Some **cars** go on roads.

Some **cars** go on tracks.

card   A card is a flat, stiff piece of paper. Often it has words and pictures on it.

Big Bird is making a birthday **card** for his friend Snuffle-upagus.

Rodeo Rosie and Bad Bart are playing a game with **cards.**

Go fish!

careful   When you are careful, you pay attention to what you are doing.

I am **careful** when I cross the street.

carpenter   A carpenter is someone who builds things with wood.

tap tap

Bert the **carpenter** uses a saw to cut the wood. He uses a hammer to pound in the nails.

carpet   A carpet is a cover for the floor.

Barkley likes to roll around on the **carpet.**

carrot   A carrot is a vegetable. Carrots are orange and grow in the ground.

Farmer Grover is pulling up some **carrots** for dinner.

carry   When you carry something, you pick it up and take it somewhere.

Herry Monster is very strong. He can **carry** a lot.

carton   A carton is a kind of container. It can hold things.

Bert is carrying the groceries in a **carton.**

castle   A castle is a very big building with tall towers and thick walls.

Come into my **castle.** But first let me count it. 1... one beautiful **castle!**

cat   A cat is a furry animal with claws.

Some **cats** are small and tame.

Some **cats** are big and wild.

catch When you catch something, you grab it as it comes to you.

Ernie can **catch** a football.

When you **catch** a cold, you get sick.

cave A cave is a big hole under the ground or in the side of a hill.

Snuffle-upagus lives in a **cave.**

Snuffle-upagus

cent One cent is the smallest amount of money you can spend. If you have a penny, you have one cent. ←—1¢

A one-**cent** cookie costs a penny.

$0.01

1¢ COOKIES

ceiling The ceiling is the part of the room you see when you look up.

Prairie Dawn is painting the **ceiling.**

center The center is the place in the middle.

A doughnut has a hole in the **center.**

cereal   Cereal is a food made from grain.

Ernie and Bert are eating **cereal** for breakfast. Bert is having oatmeal. Ernie is having crispies with milk.

certain   When you are certain about something, you are very sure of it.

Are you **certain** that Cookie Monster will want this box of cookies?

Yes, I am sure he will.

chair   A chair is a piece of furniture that you sit on. A chair has a back to lean against.

What time is it when Herry Monster sits on your **chair**?

Time to get a new **chair**!

change   When you change something, you make it different.

I, the Amazing Mumford, will now **change** this cute little kitten into a big, ferocious lion! A LA PEANUT BUTTER SANDWICHES!

Now I wonder how I can **change** this big, ferocious lion back into a cute little kitten!

chase   When you chase something, you go after it.

Whoa, Fred! Wait for me!

Marshal Grover has to **chase** his horse, Fred.

cheek   Your cheeks are the sides of your face. Look up the word face.

Roosevelt Franklin is kissing his mother on her **cheek.**

cheese   Cheese is a food made from milk.

Prairie Dawn is having a picnic. She is eating **cheese** and crackers.

chew   When you chew, you mash up food with your teeth.

Fred likes to **chew** on a carrot.

chest   Your chest is the front part of your body between your neck and your stomach. Look up the word body.

The letter G is on Super Grover's **chest**.

chest   A chest is also a kind of container. It is used to hold things.

Bert keeps his socks in a **chest** of drawers.

Herry Monster found a **chest** full of treasure.

chicken   A chicken is a kind of bird. Some chickens live on farms. Their eggs are good to eat.

I am a baby **chicken.** I am a chick.

I am the chick's father. I am a rooster.

I am the chick's mother. I am a hen.

child   A child is a young boy or girl.

Charlie is the last **child** in line. There are three **children** in front of him.

chilly When you are chilly, you are too cool to be comfortable.

It is so cold outside.
I am **chilly.**
I need my coat.

chin Your chin is the part of your face below your mouth. Look up the word face.

The Count has a beard on his **chin.**

choose When you choose, you pick one or the other.

Oh, Oscar! Which of these ice cream sundaes do you **choose**?

That's an easy **choice**! Is there anything better than cabbage ice cream with pickles and sardines?

circle A circle is a kind of shape. A circle is round.

Ernie is drawing a **circle** on the blackboard.

circus A circus is a special kind of show.

At the **circus** you can see clowns and acrobats and jugglers.

Circus animals do tricks.

city A city is a place where many people live and work.

Grover is flying his airplane over the **city.**

clean When something is clean, it is not dirty.

HOOPER'S STORE

Hi, Oscar. I **cleaned** up the sidewalk for you.

Oh, no, I can't stand a **clean** sidewalk! Where's the dirt? Where's the trash? Where's all the litter that I love?

1 2 3

climb When you climb, you move up toward the top.

The Count has to **climb** up the tree to get his cat.

clock A clock is a kind of machine that shows you what time it is.

Hi! I wonder why this **clock** is called a cuckoo **clock.**

PRESS

CUCKOO!

Oh!

close When you close something, you shut it.

Bert had to **close** the window.

AAGGH! Oscar must be cooking stinkweed for dinner.

close When two things are close, they are near each other.

Oscar's trash can is **close** to Ernie and Bert's apartment.

closet A closet is a tiny room where you can keep things—especially clothes.

clothes Clothes are what people wear. Most clothes are made from cloth.

One of these things doesn't belong here.

I wonder what that horse is doing in my **closet** with my **clothes.**

cloud A cloud is made of tiny drops of water. Clouds float in the sky.

Grover can fly his airplane through a **cloud.**

coat A coat is a piece of clothing. You wear a coat over your other clothes.

The salesman has a letter C inside his **coat.**

coin A coin is a piece of money made from metal.

A penny, a nickel, a dime, and a quarter... four **coins**!

cold When the air is cold, you feel chilly.

It's **cold** outside, Ernie. You'd better wear a sweater or you might catch a **cold.**

When you catch a **cold,** you get sick.

collection   A collection is a group of things that are alike in some way.

Hey, Ernie! Look at my paper clip **collection.**

color   Color is all around us. The grass is green. The sky is blue. Red, yellow, orange, and purple are some of the other colors you see every day.

I, the Amazing Mumford, will now pull from this perfectly empty hat... one purple thing, one red thing, one blue thing, one yellow thing, one green thing, and one orange thing.

A LA PEANUT BUTTER SANDWICHES!

THING THING THING THING THING THING

Wow! Each thing is a different **color**!

come   To come is to move from there to here.

Here I **come**! Hello, everybod-ee! I am still **coming.**

Here I go! Good-by, everybod-ee!

Grover **came,** but then he went away.

comfortable When you are comfortable, you feel good.

Big Bird is resting in his nest. He feels **comfortable.**

complain When you complain, you make a fuss about how things are.

container A container is something that can hold something else. There are many kinds of containers.

cook   When you cook, you use heat to prepare food to eat.

cook   A cook is someone who cooks.

My dad likes to **cook** spaghetti. He is a good **cook**.

cookie   A cookie is something to eat. It is usually small, flat, and sweet.

Cookies are **Cookie** Monster's favorite food.

C is for **Cookie**. That's good enough for me.

cool   When something feels cool, it is more cold than hot.

Cookies!

They are too hot. Wait until they are **cool**!

cooperate   When you cooperate, you work together with someone to do something.

Fire fighters have to **cooperate** to put out a fire.

corner   A corner is the point where two sides come together.

The **corner** of a room is the place where one wall meets another.

The **corner** of a triangle is the place where one line meets another.

A **corner** is also the place where two streets meet.

Bert was supposed to meet me at this **corner**.

costume A costume is something to wear. It can help you pretend to be someone else.

Grover's mommy made him a Halloween **costume.**

Just what I wanted— a superhero **costume!** Thank you, Mommy!

count When you count, you say numbers in order. Counting can help you find out how many things there are all together.

Here are my pet bats. How many do I have? Let us **count** them. 1, 2, 3, 4, 5, 6, 7, 8, 9 ... nine bats!

country A country is a place where many people live. Some countries are large. Some are small.

The United States of America is a large **country.**

country Country is also a name for a place that is not like the city. In the country there is usually a lot of grass and trees, but not many buildings.

I live in the **country.** I see cows and horses and ducks and a few small buildings.

I live in the city. I see cars and buses and trucks and many big buildings.

cousin The child of your aunt and uncle is your cousin.

my aunt Genevieve

my uncle Fred

me

my cousin Carol

cover When you cover people or things, you put something over them.

Ernie likes to **cover** Bert with sand at the beach.

cow A cow is an animal that usually lives on a farm and gives milk.

I am a baby **cow**. I am a calf.

I am the calf's mother. I am a **cow**.

I am the calf's father. I am a bull.

crab A crab is an animal that lives in or near the water. A crab has a hard shell, eight legs, and two claws.

I have always wondered why **crabs** have such big claws.

Ow! Now I know!

crack When something cracks, it starts to break.

Uh-oh! My wing is beginning to **crack**.

crash When one thing hits another with a loud noise, it crashes.

I am going to **crash**.

CRASH!

crawl When you crawl, you move on your hands and your knees.

It is not easy being Grover.

Grover has to **crawl** out of his airplane.

crayon A crayon is a stick of colored wax used to draw on paper.

I have a new box of **crayons.** I am drawing a picture of my friend Mr. Snuffle-upagus.

cream Cream is the thick part of milk that is made into butter.

I am churning the **cream** to make butter.

Another thing you can make from **cream** is ice **cream!**

cross When you cross something, you go from one side of it to the other.

You should always look both ways before you **cross** the street.

crowd A crowd is a lot of people together.

A **crowd** is waiting for a bus.

BUS STOP

TIMES

There is already a **crowd** on the bus.

WASH UP WITH SOAP!

BUS

cry When you cry, tears come from your eyes.

Grover spilled his milk and began to **cry.**

Don't **cry** over spilled milk, Grover, dear. I will get you some more.

cup A cup is a container to drink from. Usually it has a handle.

Snuffle-upagus has a very large **cup.**

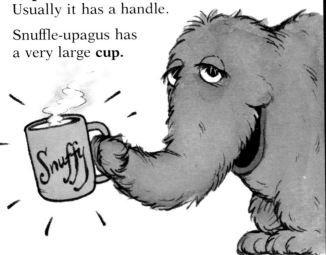

curious When you are curious, you wonder about something.

I wonder who lives in this cave.

Snuffle-upagus

Prairie Dawn is **curious.**

cut When you cut something, you divide it into pieces. Most often you use scissors or a knife.

Big Bird can **cut** out paper dolls with scissors.

Cookie the baker **cuts** his cookie dough with a knife.

I have a complaint! Why were all the wonderful words that begin with C left out of this dictionary? Where are my favorites, like crabby and creepy? What happened to chipped and crumpled? This is a crummy dictionary.

D d

A B C **D** E F G H I J K L M N O P Q R S T U V W X Y Z

dance   When you dance, you move with rhythm. Usually you dance to music.

dancer   A dancer is someone who dances.

The piper is piping. The **dancer** is **dancing**.

danger   If there is danger, there is a chance that someone may get hurt.

date   The date is the day, month, and year when something happens.

dark   When it is dark, there is no light.

daughter   A girl or a woman is the daughter of her mother and father.

dawn Dawn is the time when the sun begins to light up the sky.

Farmer Grover's rooster crows at **dawn.** It is time for Farmer Grover to wake up.

day A day is twenty-four hours long. Morning, afternoon, and night are all parts of a day.

deaf A person who is deaf cannot hear.

If you know sign language, you can talk to a **deaf** person with your hands.

decide When you decide, you make up your mind.

Cookie Monster cannot **decide** what to eat.

Cookie Monster **decided** to eat both.

decorate When you decorate something, you make it pretty.

Cookie the baker is going to **decorate** a cake.

deep When something is deep, the bottom is far below the top.

I, Grover, am standing in **deep** water.

Now I am in **deeper** water.

This is the **deepest** part of the — GLUB GLUB GLUB...

deer A deer is an animal with four legs. Most deer live in the forest. The father deer has antlers on his head.

I am a baby **deer.** I am a fawn.

I am the fawn's father. I am a buck.

I am the fawn's mother. I am a doe.

delicious When food is delicious, it tastes good.

Delicious!

deliver When you deliver something, you take it to a place or person.

I'm the Mudman. I'm here to **deliver** mud to Oscar.

dentist A dentist is someone who helps you take care of your teeth.

The **dentist** is counting and cleaning Farley's teeth.

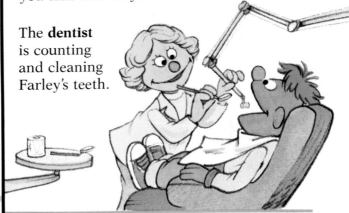

describe When you describe people or things, you tell about them.

Super Grover is fast.

Super Grover is smart.

1+1=2

Super Grover is brave.

And I am cute, too.

Fast, smart, brave, and cute are words that **describe** Super Grover.

desert   A desert is a place with very little water. Most deserts are covered with sand.

Cactus plants can grow in the **desert** because they do not need much water.

desk   A desk is a special table where you can write or draw.

Farley is sitting at his **desk** and writing a letter.

dessert   A dessert is a special food that you eat at the end of a meal.

Cookie Monster is having cookies for **dessert.**

detective   A detective is someone who tries to find the answer to a mystery.

Sherlock Hemlock is a **detective.** He is looking for clues.

dictionary   A dictionary is a book that tells the meanings of words.

This book is a **dictionary.**

Hey, Ernie, listen to this. The **dictionary** says that oatmeal is a kind of cereal made from oats.

Very interesting, Bert.

die   When things die, they stop living.

Fall is here. Soon all the leaves will **die.** The leaves on the ground are **dead.**

different When things are different, they are not the same.

Big Bird is big.
Little Bird is small.
Big Bird and Little Bird
are **different** sizes.

difficult When something is difficult, it is hard to do.

It is **difficult**
for Big Bird
to fit into
a phone booth.

This is **difficult.**

dig When you dig in the ground, you scoop up dirt.

Barkley likes
to **dig** holes.
He has already
dug three.

dime A dime is a coin. A dime is equal to ten cents. Look up the word coin.

I have
a **dime.**

I have
ten pennies.

Each of the Busby twins has ten cents.

dinner Dinner is usually the biggest meal of the day.

Cookie Monster has a well-balanced **dinner.**

dinosaur A dinosaur is a kind of animal that lived millions of years ago.

Some **dinosaurs**
were bigger than
houses. I'm glad there
are no **dinosaurs**
alive today.

direct When you direct people, you show them the way.

direction A direction is a way to go.

director A director is someone who directs.

The policewoman is a traffic **director**.
She has to **direct** the traffic in four
different **directions**.

dirt Dirt is the earth you scoop up
when you dig in the ground.

Hey, it's me,
Oscar the Grouch.
If you give me a
nice big frown, I will
show you my
dirt collection!

dirty When something is dirty, it has dirt
on it or it is not clean.

Farmer Grover
has been working
in the field.
His overalls
are **dirty**.

disagree When people disagree, they want different things or their ideas are not the same.

The Busby twins **disagree**.

disappear When something disappears, you cannot see it anymore.

I, the Amazing Mumford, will now wave my magic wand and make this rabbit **disappear**.

A LA PEANUT BUTTER SANDWICHES!

What happened to Mumphie? He **disappeared**.

disappointed You feel disappointed when something you want to happen does not happen.

Big Bird did not find any mail in his mailbox. He was **disappointed**.

discover When you discover something, you find it.

Zounds! Two suspicious-looking feet. I must **discover** whose they are.

disguise You wear a disguise to look like something or someone else.

The Big Bad Wolf is wearing a **disguise** to look like Grandma.

dish A dish is a kind of container to hold food.

Frazzle is taking a **dish** out of the cupboard.

distance Distance is the amount of space between two places or things.

The **distance** from Oscar's mud box to the fire hydrant is six feet.

divide When you divide something, you separate it into parts.

Ernie, I will **divide** this apple into two parts so that you can have half and I can have half.

Bert, I think you should have **divided** that apple into three parts.

do When you do something, you act in a certain way or you make something happen.

Every Thursday, I **do** my house-messing. When it gets too neat around here, I have to mess things up.

doctor A doctor is someone who helps people stay healthy. Doctors also help sick people get well.

The **doctor** is listening to Farley's heart with a stethoscope.

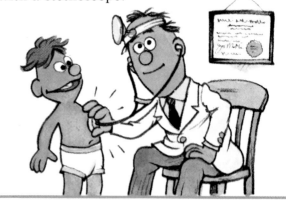

dog A dog is a kind of furry animal with a tail. Most dogs bark.

One of these things does not belong here.

A collie, a dachshund, and a poodle are all **dogs.** A turkey is a bird. The turkey does not belong.

doll A doll is a toy that looks like a person.

Herry Monster's **doll** has red hair.

dollar A dollar is an amount of money. A dollar bill is a piece of paper money equal to one hundred cents.

I, the Amazing Mumford, will now change one hundred pennies into a **dollar** bill.

Here are one hundred pennies.

Here's a **dollar.**

That's no trick! Anyone can trade a hundred pennies for a **dollar** bill.

done When something is done, it is finished.

My house-messing is **done.** Now I won't have to mess up my can until next Thursday.

door A door is used to close off the way into something.

Herry Monster, do you know how to open a **door**?

Sure.

doorknob A doorknob is a handle on a door.

No, no, Herry Monster! You are supposed to turn the **doorknob** when you open a door.

dot A dot is a very tiny round mark.

Sherlock Hemlock is looking at a **dot** on a piece of paper through his magnifying glass.

CLUE FOR THE DAY

double When something is double, there are two instead of one.

Grover the ice cream vendor gave me a **double** scoop of ice cream.

down When you go down, you move to a lower place.

Bert is going **down** the steps.

dozen When you have twelve things, you have a dozen of them.

12

Look! I have a **dozen** eggs! Will I fry them or scramble them? No! I will count them.

dragon A dragon is an imaginary animal that has wings and breathes fire.

Roosevelt Franklin is reading a book about a **dragon.**

draw When you draw, you make a picture. You can draw with a pencil or a pen or a crayon.

Roosevelt Franklin can **draw** a picture of a dragon.

drawer   A drawer is a kind of container that slides in and out of a piece of furniture. You can keep things in a drawer.

Bert is folding his socks and putting them into his **drawer.**

dream   When you dream, you see, think, and feel things while you sleep.

Cookie Monster likes to **dream** about his favorite thing.

dress   A dress is something to wear.

Betty Lou is putting on a **dress.**

dress   When you dress, you put on clothes.

I am so proud. I can **dress** myself.

drink   When you drink, you swallow a liquid.

I love to **drink** orange juice.

I love to **drink** pickle juice.

drive   When you drive something, you make it go and steer it.

driver   The driver is the one who is driving.

Grover Knover can **drive** his motorcycle over ten barrels. Grover Knover is a good **driver.**

drop   A drop is a small amount of liquid.

Sherlock Hemlock is looking at a **drop** of rain.

drop   When you drop something, you let it fall.

I, Grover, the flying letter carrier, will **drop** the mail to my friends on Sesame Street.

U.S. MAIL

drum   A drum is a musical instrument. When you play a drum, you hit it with your hands or with drumsticks.

Ernie is playing the **drum.**

dry   When something is dry, it is not wet.

It is raining, but my little umbrella keeps me **dry.**

Now I am all wet. Next time I will wear my raincoat.

dry   When you dry something, you take away the water.

Biff likes to wash the dishes. Sully likes to **dry** them.

duck A duck is a kind of bird. Ducks have webbed feet. Ducks can fly or walk or swim.

Farmer Grover's **ducks** are swimming in the pond.

I am the **duck**ling's father. I am a drake.

I am a baby **duck**. I am a **duck**ling.

I am the **duck**ling's mother. I am a **duck**.

duckie A duckie is a toy duck.

Rubber **Duckie** is a toy that floats in Ernie's bathtub.

dump The dump is a place for garbage.

dump When you dump something, you get rid of it.

The garbage truck takes the garbage to the **dump** to **dump** it.

I love to visit the **dump**! It is one of my favorite places.

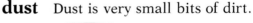

during During is a word that means between the beginning and the end.

We are about to begin our show. **During** the show, everyone must be quiet.

The Sesame Street Players

dust Dust is very small bits of dirt.

Dirt! Dump! **Dust!** This is not such a dumb dictionary after all.

Oscar loves to have **dust** in his can.

E e

A B C D **E** F G H I J K L M N O P Q R S T U V W X Y Z

each   Each means every or every one.

Each of us has a balloon. **Each** balloon is a different color.

ear   Your ear is the part of your body that you use for hearing. Look up the word body.

tic toc

Bert is holding the clock next to his **ear.** He can hear the clock ticking.

early   Early means too soon.

HOOPER'S STORE.

PARADE TODAY

Bert, did I miss the parade?

No, Ernie, you're **early.** It hasn't started yet.

early   Early can also mean near the beginning.

The sun rises **early** in the morning.

earth   Earth is the name of the planet on which we live.

Astronaut Grover can see the planet **earth.**

earth   Earth is also another word for ground.

The **earth** in Farmer Grover's garden is good for growing carrots.

easy   When something is easy, you do not have to work hard to do it.

This is hard.

This is **easy.**

eat   When you eat, you swallow food.

What did you **eat** for lunch?

I **ate** a peanut butter sandwich.

egg   An egg is a round or oval thing that holds a baby animal until it is ready to be born.

The baby robin is being born. It is hatching from its **egg.**

Aren't they cute!

eight   Eight is a number. Eight is one more than seven.

Oscar has **eight** tin cans in his used-can collection.

eighteen   Eighteen is a number. Eighteen is ten plus eight more.

Ernie has ten red marbles and eight blue marbles. He has **eighteen** marbles all together.

either   Either means one or the other.

Oh, Oscar! You can have **either** the red roses or the stinkweed.

Red roses? Yuk! I'll take the stinkweed.

elbow   Your elbow is in the middle of your arm. Your arm bends at the elbow. Look up the word body.

Betty Lou has a bandage on her **elbow.**

elephant   An elephant is a big gray animal with a long nose called a trunk.

Ⓐ

Ⓑ

Ⓒ

Which of these animals is an **elephant**?

Ⓑ

elevator   An elevator takes people or things up and down in a building.

Grover the **elevator** operator operates an **elevator.**

eleven   Eleven is a number. Eleven is ten plus one more.

Bert has ten socks that match and one sock that does not match. He has **eleven** socks all together.

empty   When something is empty, there is nothing or no one in it.

The cookie jar is full.

The cookie jar is **empty.**

end   The end is the very last part of something.

Big Bird is standing at the **end** of the line.

end   When something ends, it is over.

The play will **end** when the curtain comes down.

energy   Energy is power to do work. People and machines need energy. Energy for your body comes from food. Energy for machines can come from burning fuel or from the sun.

Farmer Grover uses **energy** from the sun to heat his henhouse.

engine   An engine is a machine that makes something go.

This tractor will not go unless I turn on the **engine.**

engineer   An engineer is someone who knows how to build machines or roads or bridges or buildings.

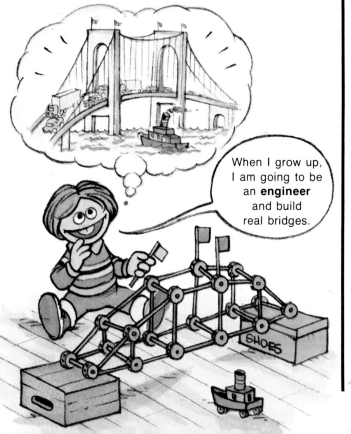

When I grow up, I am going to be an **engineer** and build real bridges.

engineer   A train engineer is someone who drives a train.

Cookie the train **engineer** is driving the Cookie Express.

enjoy   When you enjoy yourself, you have a good time.

I **enjoy** feeding pigeons.

Here, pigeons!

I **enjoy** counting pigeons. 1, 2, 3, 4, 5... five well-fed pigeons!

enough   When you have enough, you have as much as you need.

There are six grouches and six garbage cans. There are **enough** garbage cans for everyone!

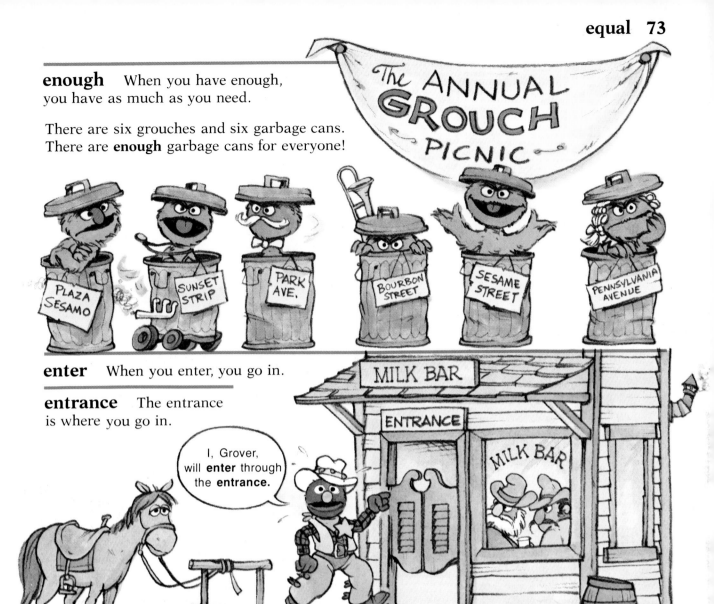

THE ANNUAL GROUCH PICNIC

PLAZA SESAMO

SUNSET STRIP

PARK AVE.

BOURBON STREET

SESAME STREET

PENNSYLVANIA AVENUE

enter   When you enter, you go in.

entrance   The entrance is where you go in.

I, Grover, will **enter** through the **entrance.**

MILK BAR

ENTRANCE

MILK BAR

envelope   An envelope is a paper container for a letter.

Big Bird has written a letter. He is putting it into an **envelope.**

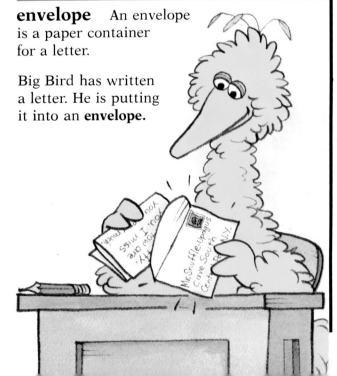

equal   When things are equal, they are the same in number or size.

I have three presents.

I have three presents.

The Busby twins have an **equal** number of presents.

equipment Equipment is a set of things you need to do a job.

Biff and Sully are carrying **equipment** to repair the street.

erase When you erase something, you wipe it away.

Baby Breeze, **erase** that picture.

teacher

eraser An eraser is something you use to erase with.

Bert has eight **erasers** in his **eraser** collection.

escalator An escalator is a stairway with moving steps. Escalators can take you up or down.

DOWN

even When two things or people are even, they are at the same level. They can also be at the same distance from a certain point.

Grover and Betty Lou are riding side by side on the **escalator**. They are **even** with each other.

even Even also means smooth, flat, or level.

Farmer Grover is raking his garden so the ground will be **even.**

ever   Ever means at any time or at all times.

As our story ends, Marshal Grover is riding into the sunset. Will he **ever** return to Sesame Gulch? Will he **ever** capture Bad Bart? Will he **ever** sit on Fred the right way?

every   Every means each one or all.

Every morning the sun comes up in the east.

except   Except means leaving out.

Everybody **except** Big Bird is in Big Bird's nest.

Hey, everybody! What about me?

excited   You feel excited when you expect something wonderful.

I wonder what is in this package. Oh, I'm so **excited**! Maybe it's a bag of birdseed or a pillow for my nest or…

exercise   When you exercise, you make your muscles work.

Exercise is good for you.

Betty Lou and Farley like to **exercise**.

exit   The exit is the way out.

The Alphabeats are leaving through the **exit.**

expect   When you expect something, you think it will happen.

expensive   When something is expensive, it costs a lot of money.

explain   When you explain something, you try to help someone else understand it.

extra   When you have an extra amount of something, you have more than you need.

eye   Your eye is a part of your face. You use your eyes for seeing. Look up the word face.

A B C D E **F** G H I J K L M N O P Q R S T U V W X Y Z

face   Your face is the front part of your head.

Can you name the parts of Bert's **face**?

eyebrow
eye
forehead
nose
cheek
ear
mouth
chin

fact   A fact is something that is true.

The tallest living animal is the giraffe.

Is that true?

It's a **fact**, Big Bird.

factory   A factory is a building where many people work together to make something.

Figgy Fizz Co. Inc.

BOTTLE CAPS

Figgy Fizz

Everyone at the Figgy Fizz **factory** has a different job.

fair   When you are fair, you try to treat everyone the same way.

That's not **fair**!

That's **fair**!

fairy A fairy is a make-believe person. Most fairies we read about have wings and magical powers.

There is a picture of a **fairy** in Big Bird's book of **fairy** tales.

A **fairy** tale is a story about **fairies** or other make-believe creatures.

fall Fall is the name of a season. Fall comes after summer.

In the **fall,** the leaves turn beautiful colors.

Fall and autumn are two different names for the same season.

fall When something falls, it drops down.

I love to watch the rain **fall** because I love to count the raindrops.

false When something is false, it is not true.

TRUE OR FALSE!

Hi, everybody! I'm Guy Smiley, everybody's favorite game show host. And here is everybody's favorite game show— TRUE OR **FALSE**?

Me called Big Bird. True or **false**?

Hi! I'm Oscar the Grouch. True or **false**?

I hate this game— true or **false**?

family   A family is a group of people who are related.

"This is my **family**."
"I'm her mother."
"I'm her father."
"I'm her sister."
"I'm her brother."

famous   When you are famous, many people know who you are.

Big Bird is a **famous** bird.

fan   A fan makes a breeze that helps to keep you cool.

"I am cooling off in front of an electric **fan**."

"I am cooling off with a paper **fan**."

far   When something is far, it is a long distance away.

The moon is very **far** from the earth.

Earth
Moon

farm   A farm is a place where people grow food and raise animals.

farmer   A farmer is someone who works on a farm.

Farmer Grover grows corn on his **farm.** He feeds the corn to his pigs.

fast   When something moves fast, it moves very quickly.

The hare runs **fast.** The tortoise walks slowly.

fasten When you fasten something, you make it hold together.

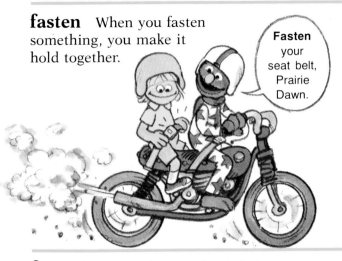

Fasten your seat belt, Prairie Dawn.

fat When something is fat, it is big around.

Some pretzels are **fat.**

Some pretzels are thin.

father A father is a man who has a child.

This is my **father**. I call him Dad. My **father** is putting a bandage on my knee. Thanks, Dad.

favorite The one that is your favorite is the one you like the best.

My **favorite** food is birdseed.

My **favorite** food is cabbage.

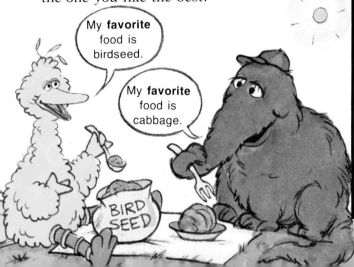

BIRD SEED

fear When you fear something, you are afraid of it.

There is nothing to **fear**. The monsters on Sesame Street are friendly.

feather A feather is something that grows on a bird. Feathers help birds to stay warm. They also help them to fly.

Aha! I have found a **feather**. I wonder where it came from.

feed When you feed people or animals, you give them food.

Bert likes to **feed** the pigeons.

feel When you feel something, you touch it. Different things feel different.

I like to **feel** a kitten's fur because it is soft.

A bug **feels** with the **feelers** on top of its head.

feel Feel also means to be or seem a certain way.

LITTLE JERRY AND THE MONOTONES SING ABOUT THEIR FEELINGS

I **feel** happy.

I **feel** sad.

I **feel** hungry.

I **feel** mad.

fence A fence is a kind of wall that is usually outdoors. A fence is usually built to keep things in or out.

I wonder why this **fence** is here.

Oh!

few Few means a small number.

Bert has a **few** bottle caps in the red box. He has many bottle caps in the blue box.

field A field is a large piece of ground where there are no buildings and usually no trees.

Farmer Grover is planting seeds in his **field.**

fifteen Fifteen is a number. Fifteen is ten plus five more.

Cookie the baker made ten round cookies and five square cookies. He made **fifteen** cookies all together.

fight When you fight, you struggle against someone or something.

The job of the fire **fighters** is to **fight** fires.

find When you find something, you discover it. Sometimes you find things by accident. Sometimes you look for something until you find it.

Egad! I, Sherlock Hemlock, have **found** a mystery. Where is this water coming from?

I will have to keep searching until I **find** the answer.

finger Your finger is a part of your hand. Most people have five fingers on each hand and ten fingers all together. Look up the word body.

How does this monster count to fifteen?

On his **fingers**!

fill When you fill a container, you put something into it until it will hold no more.

Ernie will **fill** the bathtub with water. When it is **full**, he will take a bath.

finish When you finish, you come to the end.

Cookie the baker has **finished** baking a cake.

Soon he will **finish** eating the cake.

fire Fire is flame, heat, and light caused by something burning.

fire engine A fire engine is a truck that carries fire fighters and their equipment to a fire.

fire fighter A fire fighter is someone whose job is to put out fires.

The **fire fighters** drove their **fire engine** to the **fire.**

first When something is first, it comes before all the others.

Cookie Monster is **first** in line.

COOKIES

FREE COOKIE TO **FIRST** IN LINE!

fish A fish is an animal that lives in the water. A fish breathes through special openings called gills. Most fish have fins and scales.

Bert is watching the **fish.** The **fish** are watching Bert.

fish To fish means to try to catch a fish.

Herry Monster likes to **fish.**

fit When something fits, it is the right size or shape.

five Five is a number. Five is one more than four.

Herry Monster is eating **five** carrots for lunch.

fix When you fix something, you make it right again.

Betty Lou will **fix** the broken faucet.

flag A flag is a piece of cloth. Most flags have special colors and a special meaning. Every country has its own flag.

Grover is holding the American **flag.**

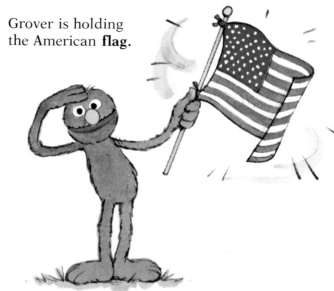

flat   When something is flat, it is not bumpy.

What do monsters eat that is square and green and **flat** as a pancake?

A square green pancake!

flavor   The flavor of something is its taste.

I love the **flavor** of chocolate ice cream.

I love the **flavor** of chocolate, too. Heh, heh. I love spinach with chocolate sauce.

float   When something floats, it stays on top of the water.

Herry's toy boat can **float** on water.

floor   The floor is the part of the room you walk on. Sometimes the floor is covered with a carpet.

What is the first thing a monster puts on when he gets out of bed in the morning?

He puts his feet on the **floor**!

flour   Flour is a powder that is made from grain. It is used to make cake, bread, and other things to eat.

Cookie the baker uses **flour** to make cookies.

flower   A flower is the part of the plant that has petals. Many flowers have sweet smells and pretty colors.

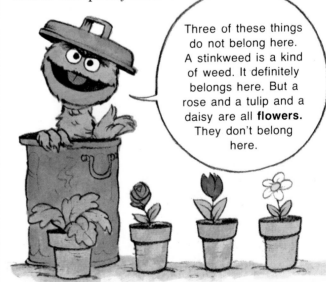

Three of these things do not belong here. A stinkweed is a kind of weed. It definitely belongs here. But a rose and a tulip and a daisy are all **flowers.** They don't belong here.

fly A fly is
a kind of insect
with wings.

Look!
There is another **fly**!
I love to count **flies**.
1, 2, 3, 4, 5…
five fabulous **flies**!
Wonderful!

fly When things fly, they move in the air.

Some birds **fly**
and some don't.

Grover likes to **fly** his airplane.

Betty Lou likes to **fly** her kite.

fly When you fly something, you make it
move in the air.

fold When you fold something, you bend
one part of it over another part.

Bert likes to
fold laundry.

follow When you follow something, you
move along behind it.

Cookie Monster will **follow**
anyone with cookies.

food Food is what we eat. All living
things need food to help them grow.

Bert is feeding the pigeons some pigeon
food. Ernie is feeding the plants some
plant **food.**

foot A foot is an amount of distance. There are twelve inches in a foot. Look up the word inch.

Bert's paper-clip chain is one **foot** long.

foot Your foot is the part of your body at the end of your leg. Look up the word body.

forehead Your forehead is the part of your face above your eyebrows. Look up the word face.

There is a fly on the Count's **foot** and a fly on his **forehead**.

forest A forest is a place where many trees grow.

Prairie Dawn is hiking through the **forest**.

forget When you forget something, you do not remember it.

Bert is going to the store. What did he **forget**? He **forgot** his pants.

fork A fork is a tool used to pick things up. Some forks are used to pick up food.

forward Forward means toward the front or the direction in which your feet are pointing.

The Monster Marching Band is marching **forward**.

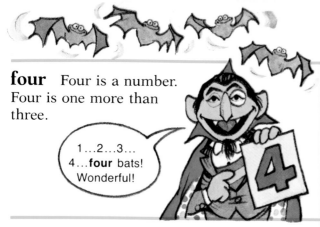

four   Four is a number. Four is one more than three.

*1...2...3... 4...**four** bats! Wonderful!*

fourteen   Fourteen is a number. Fourteen is ten plus four more.

Bert has ten small paper clips and four large paper clips. He has **fourteen** paper clips all together.

fox   A fox is a wild animal with a bushy tail.

The quick brown **fox** jumped over the lazy dog.

free   When something is free, it does not cost any money.

*Nobody wants my pickle juice even though it is **free**. I don't understand it.*

PICKLE JUICE
10¢ 5¢ FREE!

free   When you are free, you can move in any direction.

Help! I can't move.

*Ho-boy! It is good to be **free** again.*

freeze   When something freezes, it turns to ice.

*I had to wait for the pond to **freeze**. Now it is **frozen** and I can ice skate.*

friend   A friend is someone you like who likes you.

*Mr. Snuffle-upagus is my best **friend**.*

frighten When you frighten someone, you make that person afraid.

Oscar likes to **frighten** Frazzle.

frog A frog is an animal that lives in or near water. It has webbed feet and strong back legs for jumping. A baby frog is a tadpole.

I can't believe my famous uncle, Kermit the **Frog,** was ever a tadpole.

from From means out of.

Cookie Monster got some cookies **from** the cookie jar.

from From also means beginning with.

I know my letters **from** A to Z.

ABCDEFG HIJKLMN OPQRSTU VWXYZ

front The front of something is the part that usually faces forward.

Grover's airplane has a propeller in **front.**

frown When you frown, you look unhappy or angry.

I look so handsome when I **frown.**

fruit A fruit is something that grows on a plant or a tree and holds seeds. Many fruits are sweet and good to eat.

One of these things does not belong in this **fruit** bowl.

An apple, a banana, and an orange are all **fruits.** That blue, furry thing is not a **fruit.**

Cookie Monster, get your paw out of the **fruit** bowl.

fuel Fuel is something that burns to make heat or energy. Wood, coal, gas, and oil are kinds of fuel.

The fire needs more **fuel.** I, Grover, am bringing another piece of wood.

full When something is full, it holds all that it can hold.

Here is a glass of ice-cold Figgy Fizz for my old buddy Bert.

But, Ernie, this glass is almost empty. I want a **full** glass.

Here is a **full** glass, Bert.

But this glass is **full** of marbles. I can't drink marbles.

fun When something is fun, you enjoy it.

You can have a lot of **fun** with marbles.

funny When something is funny, it makes you laugh.

How do you like my Halloween costume, Ernie?

Very **funny**, Bert.

fur Fur is soft, thick hair.

Some animals are covered with **fur.**

Herry Monster's **fur** is blue.

furniture Some of the movable things in a room are called furniture. Tables, chairs, and beds are pieces of furniture.

Hey, Herry, I'm not a piece of **furniture.**

Herry Monster is moving the **furniture.**

Of all the F words, my favorite is frown. That's a fact.

G g

A B C D E F **G** H I J K L M N O P Q R S T U V W X Y Z

game   A game is something that you play in a special way.

Hi, folks! This is Guy Smiley, everybody's favorite **game** show host, bringing you everybody's favorite **game**—HIDE AND SEEK!

Four friends from Sesame Street are hiding. If you want to play this **game,** you must find them.

HIDE and SEEK!

garage   A garage is a special place used to park cars.

The Count is driving his bat car into the **garage.**

garage   A garage is also a building where mechanics repair cars.

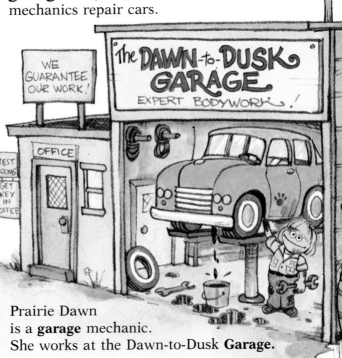

Prairie Dawn is a **garage** mechanic. She works at the Dawn-to-Dusk **Garage.**

garbage Garbage is leftover food that is thrown away.

The **garbage** collector is collecting the **garbage**. He empties the **garbage** cans into the **garbage** truck.

Beat it, buddy! This can is my home.

garden A garden is a place where someone has planted flowers or vegetables.

Farmer Grover planted six different kinds of vegetables in his **garden.**

gate A gate is a door in a fence or wall.

Herry Monster is opening the **gate.**

get When you get something, you receive it.

Oscar **gets** his mud from the Mudman.

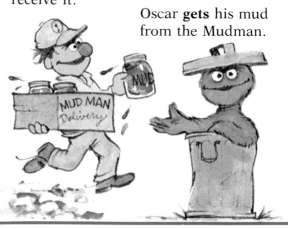

giant Giant means very big.

Big Bird found a **giant** toothbrush. It belongs to Snuffle-upagus.

gift A gift is a present.

Here, Mr. Snuffle-upagus, I made a **gift** for you.

Gee, thanks, Bird. Socks are just what I need.

giraffe A giraffe is the tallest animal in the world. It has a very long neck and eats leaves.

Is it true that a **giraffe** is the tallest animal in the world?

That's a fact.

girl A girl is a child who will grow up to be a woman.

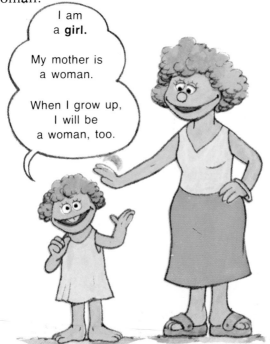

I am a **girl**.

My mother is a woman.

When I grow up, I will be a woman, too.

give When you give something to someone, you hand it to that person.

Grover bought some flowers to **give** to his mother.

Thank you, Grover. These are the most beautiful flowers you ever **gave** me.

glad When you are glad, you are happy.

I'm **glad** you're my friend, Bird.

glass Glass is hard and smooth and breakable. You can see through most glass.

Three of these things belong together. One of these things is not the same.

A mirror, a window, and a **glass** slipper are all made out of **glass**. A cowgirl boot is made out of leather. The boot does not belong.

A **glass** is something to drink from that is made out of **glass**.

glasses Glasses help people who do not see well to see better.

Mr. Chatterly wears **glasses** to help him see.

glove A glove is a cover for your hand. It helps protect your hand and keeps it warm. Most gloves have places for five fingers.

Cookie the baker wears rubber **gloves** when he washes the dishes.

glue Glue is wet and sticky and is used to join things together.

Ernie is using **glue** to put his model airplane together.

go When you go, you move from one place to another.

Here I **go**! Good-by, everybod-ee!

Where did he **go**?

He **went** that way.

Now he is **gone**.

goat A goat is an animal with hoofs and horns.

Farmer Grover's **goats** are in the vegetable garden.

I am a baby **goat**. I am a kid.

I am the kid's mother. I am a nanny **goat**.

I am the kid's father. I am a billy **goat**.

gold Gold is a heavy yellow metal. Coins and jewelry are often made of gold.

At last I have found the buried treasure! Now I can count it. One piece of **gold**, two pieces of **gold**, three pieces of **gold** ...

gone When something is gone, it is no longer there.

Zounds! The cookies are **gone**!

The plate is **gone**!

Even the table is **gone**!

good Something that is good is done well.

That is a **good** trick, Betty Lou.

good When you are happy or healthy, you feel good.

Betty Lou has lots of energy. She feels **good**.

good A good person is kind and thinks of other people.

Would you like to share my sandwich, Sully?

Biff is a **good** friend.

goose A goose is a large bird. Some geese live on farms. Some geese are wild.

I am a baby **goose.** I am a gosling.

I am the gosling's mother. I am a **goose.**

I am the gosling's father. I am a gander.

The **geese** are swimming in the lake.

grab When you grab something, you take hold of it suddenly.

Grover, **grab** your balloon before it flies away.

grain A grain is a tiny piece of something.

When I am at the beach, I can count each **grain** of sand.

grain Grain is also the food that cereal and flour are made from.

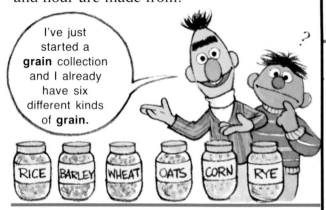

I've just started a **grain** collection and I already have six different kinds of **grain.**

RICE BARLEY WHEAT OATS CORN RYE

grandparents Your grandparents are the parents of your father or mother.

GRANDFATHER MOTHER FATHER GRANDMOTHER
GRANDMOTHER GRANDFATHER

grape A grape is a small, round fruit that grows in bunches on vines.

Betty Lou is picking **grapes.**

grass Grass is a plant that covers the ground. Some grass is short and green. Some is tall and golden.

Farmer Grover's cows are eating the **grass** in the pasture.

great When something is great, it is bigger or better than usual.

Gee, Rodeo Rosie, that's a **great** trick!

grocery store A grocery store is a place where you can buy food and supplies which are called groceries. The person who sells groceries is the grocer.

Bert is buying **groceries** from the **grocer** at the **grocery store.**

CHECK OUT

OAT MEAL OAT MEAL

Special

grouch   A grouch is someone who complains a lot.

What is **grouchier** than a **grouch**?

Two **grouches**!

ground   The ground is the solid top part of the earth.

Grover's airplane is on the **ground**.

group   A group is a collection of people or things.

A **group** of monsters is walking down the street.

grow   When something grows, it becomes bigger.

Jack's beanstalk began to **grow**, and it kept on **growing** and **growing** and **growing**.

grow   When you grow something, you put a seed or a plant in dirt and take care of it so that it will get bigger.

I like to **grow** many different kinds of plants in my backyard.

guard   A guard is someone who protects people or things.

The crossing **guard** helps the children to cross the street.

The life**guard** is **guarding** the swimmers.

guess   When you guess, you think of an answer without knowing for sure.

guest   A guest is someone who comes to visit.

Guess who will not be a **guest** for dinner again?

guitar   A guitar is a musical instrument with strings.

Cowboy Ernie is strumming his **guitar.**

Where are all the great words that begin with G—words like grimy, grubby, and grumpy?

Hh

A B C D E F G **H** I J K L M N O P Q R S T U V W X Y Z

hair Hair grows on the top of your head and on other parts of your body. Look up the word body.

My **hair** is long and straight.

My **hair** is short and curly.

Animal **hair** is sometimes called fur...

...or wool.

half A half is one of two equal parts. The two parts together make a whole thing.

Zounds! **Half** of the pie is missing!

hammer A hammer is a tool for hitting nails and other things.

Prairie Dawn is building a tree house. She is using a **hammer** to pound a nail into the wood.

hand Your hand is the part of your body at the end of your arm. Look up the word body.

Prairie Dawn is holding a **hammer** in her **hand.**

handle   The handle of something is the part that you hold on to.

Biff's lunchbox has a **handle.**

Sully's hammer has a **handle.**

handsome   When something is handsome, it is nice to look at.

I think my snuffle is very **handsome.**

hang   To hang means to be attached to something above.

Betty Lou can **hang** by her knees.

When you hang on, you hold tightly.

Hang on, Tessie!

happen   When something happens, it takes place.

Why do these things always **happen** to me?

happy   When you are happy, you feel good about things.

The Count is **happy.**

1...2... 3...4... four bats. Ha, ha, ha... I love to count bats.

hard   When something is hard, you cannot easily change its shape. When something feels hard, it does not feel soft.

Ouch! This rock is **hard.**

A sheep's wool is soft.

hard   When something is hard to do, it takes extra work or special skill. It is not easy to do.

It's easy to make cookies.

But it's **hard** to wait while they bake.

hat   A hat is something that you wear on your head.

Hi! I'm Guy Smiley, here to play—THE **HAT** GAME! Find the **hat** that belongs to each of our guests!

The HAT GAME

hatch   When baby animals hatch, they come out of eggs.

I wonder when they will **hatch.**

Oh! They are **hatching.**

Oh! They have **hatched** and they are so cute.

I **have** some new chicks. They **have** cute little yellow feathers.

Farmer Grover **had** six eggs. Now he **has** six chicks.

have   When you have something, it belongs to you.

have   Have also means to be holding or keeping something for someone else.

I think I **have** your scarf, Big Bird.

I think I **have** yours, Little Bird.

hay   Hay is a kind of grass that has been cut and dried. Cows and horses eat hay.

Farley dropped his sewing needle in a pile of **hay.**

he   He is another way to say man or boy or male animal.

Sherlock Hemlock is looking for a needle in a haystack. Do you think that **he** will find it?

head   Your head is the part of your body above your neck. Look up the word body.

Bert has a pot on his **head.**

healthy   When you are healthy, you feel well and your body works the way it should.

I do exercises to stay **healthy.**

hear   You use your ears to hear sounds.

Super Grover has super **hearing.**

I, Super Grover, can **hear** the sound of a cookie jar being opened in the next room.

heart   Your heart is inside your chest. It pumps blood to all parts of your body. Look up the word blood.

The doctor is listening to Betty Lou's **heart.** She can hear it with her stethoscope.

A **heart** is also a special shape.

heavy Something that is heavy is harder to lift than something that is light.

Say, Ernie, why is it that I am carrying the piano and you are carrying the piano stool?

Gee, Bert. I thought the piano *and* the piano stool would be too **heavy** for you.

heel Your heel is the back part of your foot. Look up the word body.

height The height of something is how tall or high it is.

The Count is measuring Big Bird's **height** from his **heel** to the top of his head.

242... 243...244... two hundred and forty-four centimeters! That is ninety-six inches.

8 ft.

heel

helicopter A helicopter is a flying machine with a large propeller on top. Helicopters can fly in any direction.

Granny Fanny Nesselrode is flying in her **helicopter**. She can see the tops of the buildings.

hello Hello is something you usually say when you greet someone.

What do you say when you meet a two-headed monster?

Hello. Hello.

What's new?

How are you?

helmet   A helmet is a hard hat that is used to protect the head.

Super Grover wears a **helmet.**

help   When you help someone, you find ways to make things easier or nicer for that person.

Super Grover likes to **help.**

When I put on my **helmet,** I change into brave and fearless... SUPER GROVER! Now I must find someone who needs my **help.**

hen   A hen is a female chicken. Some other female birds are also called hens.

Super Grover saw a **hen.**

This is boring sitting here all day keeping these eggs warm. I could use some **help.**

her   Her is another way to say woman or girl or female animal. It can also mean belonging to a woman, a girl, or a female animal.

The hen was tired of sitting on **her** eggs. Super Grover wanted to help **her.**

There is someone who needs my **help.** Down, down, and away!

HELP! HELP!

here   Here means in this place.

Here is a picture of Super Grover and the hen.

Get out of **here,** you...you... you furry blue thing!

Oh, do not thank me! I am happy to **help.** We super**heroes** live to serve.

hero   A hero is someone who is brave and fearless and very helpful.

Super Grover thinks he is a **hero.**

THE END

hide   When you hide, you stay where no one can see you. When you hide something, you put it where no one can find it.

Do you want to play **hide**-and-seek? I will **hide** and you try to find me.

high   Something that is high is farther up than something that is low.

I can reach the **high** shelf.

BIRD SEED

I can reach the low shelf.

BIRD SEED

hill   A hill is a small mountain.

Prairie Dawn is climbing up the **hill.**

SESAME STREET

him   Him is another way to say man or boy or male animal.

Herry Monster lost his doll. Betty Lou returned it to **him.**

hip   Your hips are on both sides of your body below your waist. Look up the word body.

Prairie Dawn is dancing with her hands on her **hips.**

SESAME

hippopotamus   A hippopotamus
is a big animal with a large head,
short legs, and thick skin.
It lives in a river or a lake.

Behold the
hippopotamus!
He is heavier than
the lot of us!

his   His means belonging to a man, a boy,
or a male animal.

Ernie is holding **his** bat.

hit   When you hit something, you strike it.

Ernie is going to **hit** the ball with **his** bat.

hold   When you hold something,
you take it in your hands.

Marshal Grover has to **hold** on to
Fred's tail so he won't fall off.

hold   Hold also means to keep something in place. Containers can hold many different things.

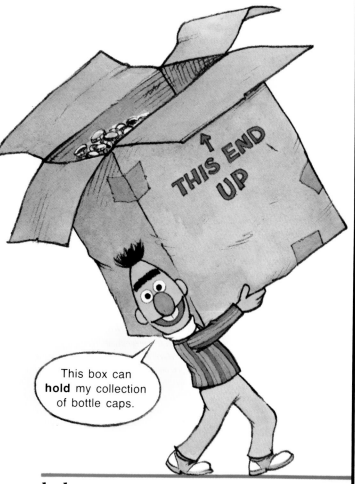

This box can **hold** my collection of bottle caps.

hole   A hole is an opening in something.

Super Grover has a **hole** in his cape.

holiday   A holiday is a special day in the year when people celebrate something. On some holidays people do not work or go to school.

The Fourth of July is a **holiday.** On the Fourth of July we celebrate the birthday of the United States.

home   Your home is the place where you live.

Ernie and Bert's **home** is in an apartment house.

Big Bird's **home** is a nest.

honey Honey is a sweet syrup made by bees.

The queen is in the parlor eating bread and **honey.**

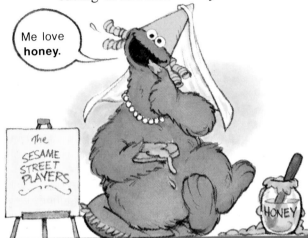

Me love **honey.**

The SESAME STREET PLAYERS

HONEY

hook A hook is used to hold things, catch things, or fasten things. A hook is bent at one end.

Can you find three kinds of **hooks** in this picture?

hop When you hop, you jump up and down.

Grover loves to **hop.** He is playing **hop**scotch.

Do you see how I am **hopping** from square number one to square number two?

HOME

horn A horn is a musical instrument that you blow into.

horn A horn is also something that makes a loud noise to warn people.

horn The horns on the heads of some animals are made of bone or hair and are used for protection.

I, the Amazing Mumford, will now pull from this perfectly empty hat three different things with the same name.

A LA PEANUT BUTTER SANDWICHES!

Now where is that other kind of **horn**?

It's right behind you, Mumphie!

horse A horse is an animal with four long legs, a mane, and a tail. People can ride on horses.

I am a baby **horse.** I am a foal.

I am the foal's mother. I am a mare.

I am the foal's father. I am a stallion.

Whoa, Fred!

Some **horses** can run very fast.

hospital A hospital is a building where people go when they need special help from doctors.

I'm in the **hospital** because the doctor took out my tonsils.

hot When something is hot, it is very, very warm.

Oh! This porridge is **hot**!

What a **hot** day!

THE SESAME STREET PLAYERS

GOLDILOCKS AND THE 3 BEARS

hotel A hotel is a building where people pay money to sleep and eat when they are away from home.

Granny Fanny Nesselrode is going to stay at the Sesame Gulch **Hotel**.

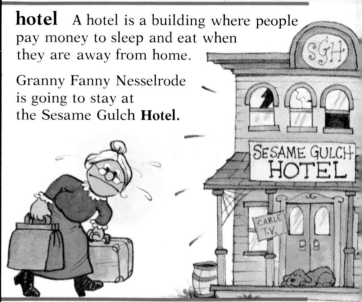

SGH

SESAME GULCH HOTEL

CABLE T.V.

hour An hour is an amount of time. An hour is sixty minutes long.

Hey, Bert. It takes one **hour** for my pet fish to swim a hundred laps.

Are you through with the bathtub, Ernie?

house   A house is a building to live in. Some houses are big enough for only one family. Apartment houses are big enough for many families.

I live in a **house.**

I live in an apartment **house.**

I live in a bird**house.**

how   How means in what way or in this way.

Can you tell me **how** to get to Sesame Street?

Sure. Follow that bird.

hug   When you hug someone, you put your arms around that person.

huge   When something is huge, it is very, very big.

Snuffle-upagus is too **huge** to **hug.**

hundred   One hundred is a number. One hundred is one more than ninety-nine.

There are one **hundred** cents in a dollar.

97...98... 99...100... one **hundred** cents! Wonderful!

hungry   When you feel hungry, you want to eat.

Biff and Sully are **hungry.** They are having lunch.

hunt When you hunt for something, you look for it.

hurry When you hurry, you move faster than usual.

Sherlock, I lost Rubber Duckie.

Have no fear. I, Sherlock Hemlock, the world's greatest detective, will **hunt** for it.

Please **hurry**, Sherlock. I can't take my bath without Rubber Duckie.

hurt When you hurt, you feel pain. Frazzle bumped his foot. His foot **hurts.**

husband A husband is a man who is married.

I am married to him. He's my **husband.**

I am married to her. She's my wife.

This dictionary has left out a good H word—heap!

Some of my favorite heaps are junk heaps, garbage heaps, and rubbish heaps.

I i

I   I is a word you use when you are talking or thinking about yourself.

ice   Ice is frozen water.

Herry Monster is skating on the **ice**.

I like to skate on the **ice**.

I think he should be more careful.

I think this **ice** is cold.

ice cream   Ice cream is a sweet, frozen food made with cream and sugar.

idea   An idea is a thought in someone's mind.

Now, what shall I do with this extra **ice cream** cone?

I have a good **idea**.

ICE CREAM

if If means supposing that.

imagination You use your imagination to think of things that are not right in front of you or things that are not real.

If Mr. Snuffle-upagus had wings, he would be a snuffle-bird.

Big Bird has a good **imagination.**

immediately Immediately means right now.

Operator? Get me the Mudman **immediately**! I'm out of mud.

important When something is important, it matters very much to someone.

Mud is **important.**

Counting is **important.**

Clues are **important.**

impossible When something is impossible, it cannot be done.

I would like a peanut butter sandwich without any bread.

That is **impossible**, sir! You cannot make a sandwich without bread.

in In means within or surrounded by. In means not out.

Little Bird is **in** his nest.

Cookie Monster has his hand **in** the cookie jar.

inch An inch is an amount of distance. There are twelve inches in a foot.

The six of us together are an **inch** long.

1 in.

insect An insect is a tiny animal with six legs. Some insects have wings. Some do not.

Butterfly
Ant
Ladybug
Dragonfly

My favorite **insect** is the ladybug.

inside   Inside means within.

I am hiding **inside** Mumphie's hat.

instead   Instead means in place of.

I, the Amazing Mumford, will now pull from this perfectly empty hat a beautiful silk scarf.

A LA PEANUT BUTTER SANDWICHES!

That's strange! I pulled out a rabbit **instead** of a scarf.

interesting   When something is interesting, it holds your attention.

That's an **interesting** rock, Bert.

Yes, it has many beautiful colors in it, Ernie.

Gee, Bert. I just thought it was **interesting** because there's a great big spider crawling on it.

into   When you go into something, you enter it.

Farmer Grover is driving his tractor **into** the barn.

invisible   When something is invisible, you cannot see it.

Air is all around you, but it is **invisible.**

invite   When you invite someone, you ask that person to come for a visit or to do something with you.

invitation   An invitation is used to ask someone to a party or a special occasion.

I will **invite** five guests to Fatatatita's birthday party. Here are the **invitations.** Let me count them.... 1, 2, 3, 4, 5! Wonderful!

iron An iron is a tool used to smooth the wrinkles out of clothes. An iron must be heated before it can be used.

Bert is **ironing** his pigeon costume with an **iron.**

is Grover's favorite story **is** about Super Grover.

island An island is a piece of land that is surrounded by water.

Once upon a time Super Grover was flying over a small **island.**

That little boy on the **island** is about to walk into a patch of poison ivy. I must stop him. Down, down, and away!

it It is a word you use when you are talking or thinking about a thing.

Look at all that poison ivy. I will be careful not to step in **it.**

Don't touch **it!** Don't walk in **it!** Don't pick **it!** Don't…

…land in **it!**

Poison ivy will give you an **itch.**

itch An itch is a feeling that makes you want to scratch your skin.

Super Grover has an **itch.**

THE END

I see that an important I word is missing—insult. An insult is something you say that is not kind—such as, turn the page immediately. You are bothering me.

A B C D E F G H I J K L M N O P Q R S T U V W X Y Z

jacket A jacket is a short coat.

jar A jar is a kind of container that is usually made of glass. It has a large opening at the top.

Oscar keeps his pickles in a **jar.**

job A job is work that you do. Most people are paid money for doing their jobs.

join When you join things, you put them together.

Let's all **join** hands and make a circle.

join When you join a group, you become part of it.

If you **join** the Pigeon Lovers' Club, you can wear one of these nifty jackets.

The PIGEON LOVERS' CLUB

joke A joke is something you say or do that is funny.

Hey, Ernie. Did you take a bath this morning?

No, Bert. Is there one missing? Hee hee!

That's a very funny **joke**, Ernie! Now clean up your mess!

juice Juice is the liquid that comes out of a fruit or vegetable.

Betty Lou is thirsty. She is drinking a glass of orange **juice**.

glug

glug

jump When you jump, both of your feet leave the ground at the same time.

Who can **jump** higher than a house — Grover or Herry Monster?

Both of us can! Houses can't **jump**.

jungle A jungle is a place full of trees and vines. A jungle is usually warm and damp.

Do you know why I love the **jungle**? The **jungle** is full of interesting animals to count. 1, 2, 3, 4...four interesting animals!

junk   Junk is old or broken things that are usually thrown away.

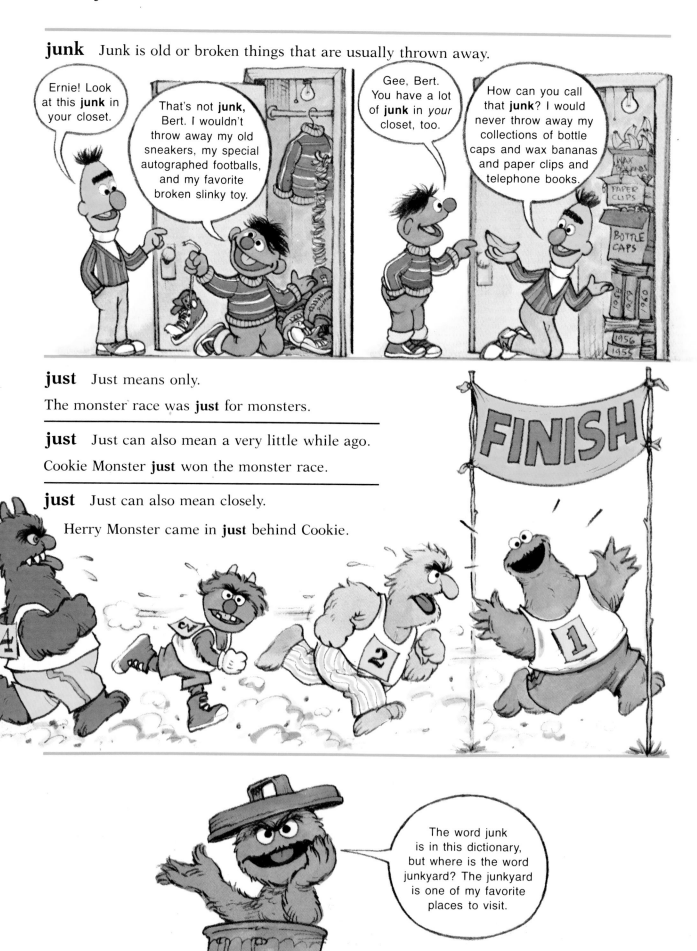

just   Just means only.

The monster race was **just** for monsters.

just   Just can also mean a very little while ago.

Cookie Monster **just** won the monster race.

just   Just can also mean closely.

Herry Monster came in **just** behind Cookie.

Kk

A B C D E F G H I J **K** L M N O P Q R S T U V W X Y Z

kangaroo   A kangaroo is an animal that has strong back legs for jumping. A mother kangaroo carries her baby in a pouch.

keep   When you keep something, you have it. Sometimes you hold it and sometimes you put it in a special place.

keep   When you keep doing something, you go on doing it.

key   A key is something that is used to open a lock.

keyhole   A keyhole is an opening for a key.

The castle door was locked. Prince Charming put the **key** into the **keyhole.**

kick   When you kick something, you hit it with your foot.

Ernie likes to **kick** his football.

Farmer Grover's cow **kicked** over the milk pail.

kid   Kid means young goat. In everyday talk, kid is used to mean child.

Did you know that a **kid** can be a young goat or a child?

You're **kidding**!

Someone who is **kidding** is joking.

kill   When you kill something, you make it die.

Wow, I can **kill** seven in one blow!

The little tailor **killed** seven flies with a fly swatter.

kind When you are kind, you are friendly and helpful.

Big Bird dropped his groceries.
Betty Lou helped him pick them up.
That was a **kind** thing to do.

kind Kind also means sort or type.

> What **kind** of sandwich would you like, sir?

> I'll have a peanut butter and jelly sandwich.

> What **kind** of peanut butter — crunchy or plain? What **kind** of jelly — grape or gooseberry? What **kind** of bread …

> This is ridiculous! Just bring me an ordinary peanut butter and jelly sandwich on a plate.

> Very well, sir! What **kind** of plate?

kindergarten Kindergarten is the class at school that comes before first grade.

Farley is helping the **kindergarten** teacher. He is passing out the scissors and paste.

king A king is a man who rules a country.

King Cookie is sitting on his throne.

> Me proclaim today National Cookie Day!

kiss When you kiss, you touch a person with your lips. A kiss shows love or friendship.

Betty Lou is going to **kiss** Grover.

kitchen   A kitchen is a room where food is cooked.

Bert is in the **kitchen** cooking oatmeal.

kite   A kite is a toy made of paper, plastic, or wood. It flies in the air on the end of a long string.

Big Bird is flying a **kite.**

kitten   A kitten is a young cat.

My cat, Fatatatita, has **kittens.** Not only are they adorable, but I can count them. 1, 2, 3, 4, 5, 6… six **kittens**!

knee   The knee is the middle part of your leg. Your leg bends at the knee. Look up the word body.

Betty Lou has a bandage on her **knee.**

knife   A knife is a tool that is used to cut things. It has a handle and a blade.

Waiter! This **knife** does not cut very well. Please bring me something a little sharper.

Right away, sir!

knock   When you knock, you hit your knuckles against something to make a noise.

Herry Monster is going to **knock** on Betty Lou's door.

Next time, Herry, don't **knock**. Use the doorbell.

knot   A knot is made by tying together pieces of one or more ropes, ribbons, or strings.

I, the Count, am tied up with ropes. Will I escape? Of course! But, first, let me count the **knots** in the ropes! 1 **knot**, 2 **knots**. Isn't this fun? 3 **knots**, 4 **knots**...

know   When you know something, you are sure of it.

My address is 123 Sesame Street.

Farley **knows** his address.

koala   A koala is a small furry animal with big ears and no tail. A koala looks like a little bear, but it is not a bear.

Koalas live in eucalyptus trees and are very shy.

Keep is my favorite word that begins with K. Can you guess why?

KEEP OUT!

KEEP OFF!

KEEP AWAY!

KEEP QUIET!

Ll

A B C D E F G H I J K **L** M N O P Q R S T U V W X Y Z

ladder A ladder is something that you can climb to reach high places. A ladder has steps that are called rungs.

Fire fighter Ernie is climbing a **ladder.**

lake A lake is water with land all around it. A lake is larger than a pond.

Prairie Dawn is paddling her canoe on the **lake.**

land Land is the part of the earth that is not water. Another word for land is ground.

I can travel on **land**…

On water…

And in the air.

land When something lands, it comes down to the ground.

Grover's airplane is going to **land.**

language Language is what we use to say things to other people. When two people understand each other's words, they know the same language.

Cookie Monster can say COOKIE in five different **languages.**

Cookie
(English).

Galleta
(Spanish).

Biscotto
(Italian).

Biscuit
(French).

餅乾

Bǐng gān
(Chinese).

large Large means big.

Marshal Grover ordered a small glass of milk for himself and a **large** glass of milk for Fred.

last When something is last, it comes after all the others.

Cookie Monster is the **last** in line. He wishes he were first.

late When you are late, you come after the time that you were supposed to.

You're **late** for our party, Connie!

I'm sorry. I couldn't find my broom.

HAPPY HALLOWEEN

late Late can also mean near the end.

The party ended **late** at night. Everyone had a good time.

later Later means after now.

Hey, Bert! Do you want a banana?

Later, Ernie! Right now I'm busy working on my bottle cap collection.

laugh   When you laugh, your whole face smiles and you make ha-ha sounds.

laundry   Laundry is all the clothes that need to be washed or the clothes that have just been washed.

Ernie and Bert are doing their **laundry.**

lay   When you lay something down, you put it down.

Bart **laid** his cards on the table.

lazy   Someone who is lazy does not want to work or to play.

The cat and the pig and the mouse are **lazy.**

lead   When you lead, you show others the way by going with them or in front of them.

leader   A leader is someone who leads.

leaf   A leaf is a thin, flat green part of a tree or a plant. It grows at the end of a branch or a stem.

learn When you learn, you find out something that you did not know before.

*I had to **learn** to use a lasso.*

*I am **learning** how to use a lasso, too.*

*I have a lot more to **learn.***

leave When you leave, you go away.

When you leave something behind, it does not go with you.

When you leave something alone, you do not touch it or bother it.

*Come on, Bert. It's time to **leave** for the show.*

*Do you think we should **leave** these cookies here?*

__Leave__ them alone, Ernie. We don't have time to put them away.

LATER

left When something is left, it is still there after all the others are gone.

Cookie Monster ate almost all of the cookies. There is only one **left.**

left Left is also a direction. It is the opposite of right.

*Now let me see. Should I turn **left** or right?*

If I were Goldilocks, I would turn around and go home.

HOUSE of the THREE BEARS

HOUSE of the BIG BAD WOLF

LEFT

RIGHT

leg   Your leg is the part of your body between your hip and your foot. Look up the word body.

Bert's **legs** are longer than Ernie's **legs.**

Ernie, I think you are wearing my pants.

length   The length of something is how long it is from one end to the other.

The **length** of this straw is eight inches.

The **length** of a story is its number of pages or how much time is needed to read or tell it.

Look up the word inch.

less   Less means not as much.

I have **less** milk than Bart has.

I have the **least** amount of milk.

let   When you let something happen, you allow it to happen.

Let the balloon fly away!

Okay. I **let** it go.

letter   A letter is a mark that stands for a sound. There are twenty-six letters in the alphabet. You can put letters together to make words. Look up the word alphabet.

letter   A letter is also a message that you write on paper and give or mail to someone.

I, the Amazing Mumford, will now pull from this perfectly empty hat two different things that have the same name.

A LA PEANUT BUTTER SANDWICHES!

librarian A librarian is someone who works in a library.

library A library is a room or building where books are kept. You can borrow books from a library.

Farley went to the **library.** The **librarian** helped him find a book about dragons.

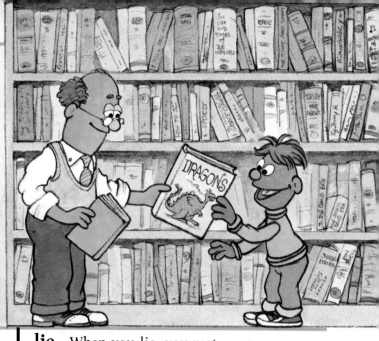

lick When you lick something, you touch it or taste it with your tongue.

Lasso Louise likes to **lick** luscious lollipops.

Say that ten times, fast.

lid A lid is a cover.

The **lid** to Oscar's garbage can is on his head.

lie When you lie, you rest on your stomach or back or side.

Barkley likes to **lie** near Big Bird's nest.

lie A lie is something that is not true.

Hey, Bert, there's a big ugly monster with two heads and four arms and eight legs, and he's standing right behind you.

You can't scare me, Ernie. I know that's a big **lie.**

Gee, Bert, how did you know I wasn't telling the truth?

Because the monster is standing behind *you,* not me!

lift When you lift something, you pick it up.

Herry Monster can **lift** a crane.

A crane can **lift** Herry Monster.

light When there is light, it is not dark and you can see. Something that gives light is sometimes called a light.

In the daytime, the sun gives us **light**.

At night, when it is dark, we can turn on electric **lights**.

light When you light something, you set it on fire.

Mommy, after you **light** the candles on my birthday cake, I will blow them out.

Make a wish first, dear.

light When something is light, it is not heavy.

A feather is **light**. It is easy to carry.

A big rock is heavy. It is not easy to carry.

lightning

Lightning is a flash of light you see in the sky.

Sometimes there is **lightning** during a rainstorm.

1 ... one bolt of **lightning**!

BOOM!

like

When you like someone or something, that person or thing makes you feel good.

I really **like** Rubber Duckie.

like

When one thing is like another thing, they are the same in some way.

What is **like** a big red furry monster with horns?

Another big red furry monster with horns!

line

A line is a long, thin mark.

Lines can be straight or curved or wiggly or crooked.

line

When people or things are in a line, they are behind or next to each other. They are in a row.

There is a **line** of people waiting to see the new movie.

TICKETS

lion

A lion is a big, wild cat that roars.

I am a baby **lion**. I am a cub.

I am the cub's mother. I am a **lion**ess.

I am the cub's father. I am a **lion**.

A group of **lions** is called a pride. Grown-up male **lions** have manes. **Lion**esses do not.

liquid   A liquid is something that is wet and can be poured.

Three of these things belong together. One of these things is not the same.

Orange juice, milk, and water are all kinds of **liquids.** A loaf of bread is not wet and cannot be poured. The loaf of bread does not belong.

listen   When you listen, you pay attention to the sounds you hear.

Hey, everyone! **Listen** to Little Jerry and the Monotones.

little   Something that is little needs less room than something that is big. It is small, not large.

How do you become a big hairy monster?

You start out as a **little** hairy monster—and then you grow!

live   To live somewhere means to have your home in that place.

I **live** in a garbage can. Slimey **lives** in a box. We both **live** on Sesame Street.

lock   A lock is something that keeps something else from being opened. You usually need a key to open a lock.

lock   When you lock something, you fasten it with a lock.

Sherlock Hemlock always **locks** his trunk with a big **lock.**

lonely   When you feel lonely, you wish you had someone to be with.

It's **lonely** at the top.

long When something is long, the beginning is far from the end.

When something takes a long time, there is a lot of time between the beginning and the end.

Lasso Louise has a **long** lasso.

look When you look, you pay attention to the things you see.

loose When something is loose, it is not tight.

Farley put on his father's shoes.
They are **loose.**

lose When you lose something, you cannot find it.

lost When something is lost, you cannot find it.

loud When something is loud, it makes a lot of sound.

That's too **loud**, Oscar!

What?

I said, THAT'S TOO **LOUD**, OSCAR!

If you'd stop yelling, Betty Lou, we could have some peace and quiet around here.

love When you love someone, you care about that person very much.

I **love** you, Mommy.

I **love** you, too, Grover, dear.

Sometimes when you like something very much, you say you **love** it.

I just **love** carrots.

lunch Lunch is the meal that you eat in the middle of the day.

Biff and Sully are going to eat **lunch**. Biff's **lunch**box is empty.

I thought I saw something blue and furry with funny eyes go by.

low Something that is low is close to the ground.

I am flying high.

I am flying **low**.

Whoops! I am flying too **low**.

One of my favorite L words is litter. I like litter because litter is trash.

Mm

A B C D E F G H I J K L **M** N O P Q R S T U V W X Y Z

machine   Machines are built by people to do special kinds of work.

This **machine** makes mud.

I'm **mad**. I'm really **mad**.

DIRT 100% PURE

mad   When you are mad, you do not like what has happened. You are angry.

magic   Magic is a way of doing something that seems to be impossible. Magicians, witches, and fairies use magic to make amazing things happen.

Amazing Mumford the **magician** does **magic** tricks.

I, the Amazing Mumford, will make this monster disappear.

A LA PEANUT BUTTER SANDWICHES!

That is **magic**!

mail   Mail is the letters and packages that are sent from one place to another.

Big Bird is dropping his **mail** into the **mail**box.

The **mail** carrier is putting the **mail** into his **mail**bag.

The **mail** carrier is delivering the **mail** to Granny Bird.

make Make means to put together or cause something to happen.

Cookie Monster loves to **make** cookies. Today he **made** twelve cookies and one mess.

make-believe When something is make-believe, it is imaginary. It is not real.

man A man is a grown-up boy.

There is one **man** in the elevator.

many Many means a lot of people, things, or animals.

There are **many** monsters in the elevator.

map A map is a special kind of picture that shows where places are.

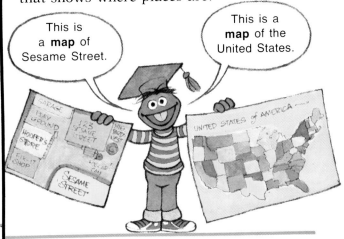

march When you march, you walk with rhythm in steps of the same size.

mark A mark is a line, spot, dent, or sign on something. A mark can be made by accident or on purpose.

marry   When two people marry, they become husband and wife.

The monsters are getting **married.**

*Will you **marry** me?*

Why not?

I now pronounce you husband and wife.

I just love weddings!

mask   A mask is something you wear over your face.

Farley and Betty Lou are wearing **masks.**

Trick or treat!

match   A match is a thin stick with a special end that is used to make a flame.

*I never play with **matches.** **Matches** can be dangerous.*

match   When two things match, they are the same in a certain way.

THE MATCHING GAME!

*And now folks, it's time for— THE **MATCHING** GAME! Each one of our contestants is holding a shape. All you have to do is find the shapes that **match.***

may May means allowed to.

maybe Maybe means possibly.

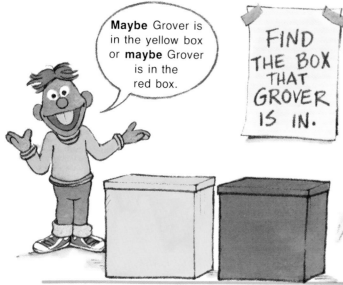

me Me is a word you use when you are talking or thinking about yourself.

meal A meal is all the food that is served when it is time to eat. You usually eat three meals a day—breakfast, lunch, and dinner.

mean When someone is mean, that person does or says things that are not kind or friendly.

mean What you mean is what you want to show by your words or your actions.

measure When you measure something, you find out how long or how heavy or how much it is.

I can **measure** my height.

I can **measure** my weight.

I can **measure** a cup of flour for baking cookies.

FLOUR

mechanic A mechanic is someone who uses tools to make or repair machines. Look up the word tool.

The Count's car is broken. The **mechanic** is trying to fix it.

23

medicine When you are sick, you sometimes use medicine to make you well.

Take your **medicine,** dear, like a good monster!

meet When you meet someone, you get together with that person.

I'm happy to **meet** you.

melt When something melts, it turns to liquid.

It is a warm day. The snow monster is starting to **melt.**

mess When things are dirty or out of place, we say they are a mess. When something is a mess, it is not neat.

I don't know anyone who can make a bigger **mess** than you, Oscar.

Gee thanks, Betty Lou. That's the nicest thing you've ever said to me.

metal   Metal is the hard stuff that some things are made of.
Iron, gold, silver, and tin are kinds of metal.

Keys are made of **metal.**

Coins are made of **metal.**

Cans are made of **metal.**

middle   The middle is the place between
the beginning and the end. The middle is
also the place that is the same distance
from all the sides. It is the center.

Three people are standing at the milk bar.
Marshal Grover is in the **middle.**

Big Bird drew a circle with chalk.
Little Bird is standing in the **middle.**

midnight   Midnight is twelve o'clock
at night.

Dum de dum de dum.
Time for my
midnight snack!

milk   Milk is a liquid food that comes
from cows and other animals. Milk is good
to drink.

Farmer Grover's pail is full of **milk.**
He has just **milked** his cow.

mind Your mind thinks and knows and remembers and feels.

Everyone at the bus stop is thinking of something different. Three different **minds** are thinking three different thoughts.

To **mind** means to care.

Do you **mind** if I borrow your dictionary?

mine Mine means belonging to me.

This towel is yours. The other towel is **mine.**

minute A minute is a small amount of time. There are sixty seconds in a minute. There are sixty minutes in an hour.

Waiter, you have exactly one **minute** to bring my milk.

Whoa, Bossie!

minus Minus means take away or subtract.

Three **minus** one is two.

mirror A mirror is a glass in which you can see yourself.

Egad! A suspicious-looking person! I wonder who he is.

Sherlock, that is *you* in the **mirror.**

miss   When you miss something, you do not hit it or find it or meet it or see it or hear it.

Keep your eye on the ball, Ernie, or you'll **miss** it.

Hurry, Sherlock, or you will **miss** the train.

I can't leave now. I'm looking for my **missing** ticket.

miss   When you miss someone, you feel sorry that person is not with you.

What's the matter, Big Bird?

I **miss** Mr. Snuffle-upagus.

mistake   When you make a mistake, you do something wrong.

I think we made a **mistake**, Sully.

mitten   A mitten is a cover for your hand to keep it warm. A mitten has a place for your thumb and a place for your other fingers.

Farley is wearing red **mittens.**

mix   When you mix things, you put them together.

You **mix** the potion while I read the recipe. Let's see... two toadstools, three bat wings...

money Money is what we use to buy things.

Hey, kid. Would you like to buy an M? It costs only nine cents.

I don't have enough **money.** I have only six cents.

You're in luck. That's exactly what this wonderful W costs.

monkey A monkey is a hairy animal with two arms and two legs. Most monkeys have long tails.

Do you know what is more fun than a barrel of **monkeys**?

Counting the **monkeys** in a barrel!

monster A monster is a large or strange living thing.

The **monsters** on Sesame Street are furry and friendly.

month A month is an amount of time that lasts about thirty days. There are twelve months in a year. Each month has a special name.

Thirty days hath September, April, June, and November. All the rest have thirty-one, Excepting February alone, And that has twenty-eight days clear, And twenty-nine in each leap year.

moon The moon is the earth's closest neighbor in space. You can sometimes see it in the sky.

Isn't the **moon** beautiful?

Grover the astronaut is on the **moon.**

Isn't the earth beautiful?

mop A mop is made of yarn or sponge that is fastened to a long stick. A mop is used for cleaning floors.

Bert is using a **mop** to **mop** the floor.

more More means a larger amount.

You have **more** cookies than I do, Ernie.

That's true, Bert. But Cookie Monster has **more** cookies than *I* do. He has the **most**.

morning The morning is the first part of the day.

RING!

Oh! Time for my **morning** snack.

mother A mother is a woman who has a child.

Grover's **mother** is reading a bedtime story to Grover.

Once upon a time…

motor A motor is an engine.

Grover Knover's **motor**cycle has a **motor**.

mountain A mountain is a part of the earth that is higher than the land around it.

I, Grover Knover, am climbing this very high **mountain**. Why? Because it is here.

mouse A mouse is a small, furry animal with a long tail.

If you have one **mouse**…

And someone gives you another **mouse**…

You have two **mice**.

mouth Your mouth is a part of your face. You eat, drink, and speak through your mouth. Look up the word face.

Hello, everybod-ee! I am here to tell you about the **mouth**. I am using my **mouth** to talk.

move   When you move, you go from one place to another place.

When you move something, you take it from one place to another place.

Sometimes the word move is used to mean changing the place where you live.

The **movers** are **moving** the country mouse to the city.

I think I'd like to **move** to the city.

CHEEZY MOVERS INC.

Ernie, let's **move** to another seat. I can't see the movie.

Prairie, please **move** your coat so I can sit in that seat.

That's not my coat. It's Cookie Monster sleeping.

zzz

movie   A movie is moving pictures that you watch on a screen. A movie usually tells a story.

Bert and Ernie are watching a **movie.**

much   Much means a great amount.

THE SESAME STREET THEATER

NOW PLAYING

THE COUNTRY MOUSE MOVES TO THE CITY

Did you like the **movie,** Bert?

I liked it very **much.**

EXIT

mud   Mud is soft, wet dirt.

Who stepped in my box of **mud**?

Don't worry, Oscar. I will solve the mystery. I will look for someone with **muddy** shoes.

FRESH MUD

muscle   A muscle is a part of your body that can stretch and pull tight to make your body move. You have many muscles inside your body.

Herry Monster uses his **muscles** to lift the barbell.

music   Music is pleasing sound that is played or sung by people. Different people like different kinds of music.

Everyone at the party is listening to the **music.**

Stop making that terrible noise!

Terrible noise? This is **music** to my ears.

must   Must means have to.

I **must** find the person who is wearing muddy shoes. Then I will know who stepped in Oscar's mud box.

my   My is another way of saying belonging to me.

Egad! **My** shoes are covered with mud. *I* am the person who is wearing muddy shoes.

I'll just sit down here and clean them off.

myself   Myself is a word that is sometimes used instead of me or I.

mystery   A mystery is something that you do not understand and try to figure out.

I found the mud on my shoes. I, **myself,** am the one who stepped in your mud box, Oscar. The **mystery** is solved.

Good, because I have another **mystery** for you to solve. Someone *sat* in my mud box.

Some of my favorite M words are missing from this dictionary— messy, moldy, and mushy. Do you know what I wish? I wish *I* were missing from this dictionary.

Nn

nail   A nail is a long, thin piece of metal that can be hammered into wood.

Prairie Dawn is making a wagon.

This **nail** will hold two pieces of my wagon together.

nail   Your nails are the hard coverings that grow on the ends of your fingers and toes.

Biff is cutting his **nails.**

name   A name is the word you use for a person, place, or thing.

Hi! My **name** is Miss Muffet. This is my pet spider. His **name** is Stanley.

nap   When you take a nap, you sleep for a small amount of time.

Snuffle-upagus is taking a **nap.**

narrow   Narrow means not wide.

Sully, that board is too **narrow.** Find one that's wider.

near   Near means close to.

Marshal Grover is **near** the cactus. Fred is far away.

neat Neat means not messy.
Ernie's closet is messy.
Bert's closet is **neat.**

neck Your neck is
the part of your body
between your head
and your shoulders.
Look up the word body.

Ernie,
I think you
have my scarf
around your
neck.

need When you need something, you
cannot do without it.

needle A needle is a long, thin tool used
for sewing. A needle has a small hole at one
end and a sharp point at the other.

Super Grover **needs** a **needle** and thread to
sew up a hole in his cape.

neighbor A neighbor is someone who lives near you.

neighborhood Your neighborhood is the place where you and your neighbors live.

We are all
neighbors.
We all live
in the same
neighborhood.

nephew If you are a boy, you are your aunt and uncle's nephew.

nest A nest is a thing made by birds or other animals to hold their babies.

A baby bird must learn to fly before it leaves its **nest.**

never Never means not at any time.

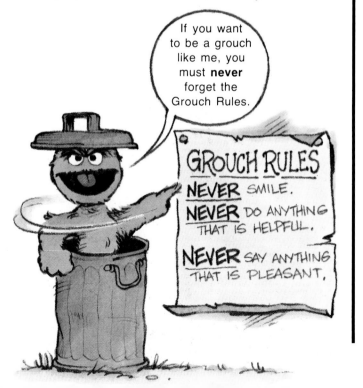

new When something is new, it has just been made or has never been used.

Goldilocks broke Baby Bear's chair.

Papa Bear made Baby Bear a **new** chair.

newspaper A newspaper is one or more sheets of paper printed to tell about the new things that have happened.

next   Next means nearest to or beside.

next   Next also means the following one.

Betty Lou is standing **next** to Farley.

We missed the bus. We'll have to take the **next** one.

nice   Something that is nice is pleasing.

Everyone likes Barkley because he is a **nice** dog.

nickel   A nickel is a coin. A nickel is worth five cents. Look up the word coin.

Each of the Busby twins has five cents.

I have a **nickel.**

I have five pennies.

nickname   A nickname is a special name that you use in place of a real name.

His real name is the Amazing Mumford, but I call him Mumphie.

Mumphie is my **nickname.**

niece   If you are a girl, you are your aunt and uncle's niece.

She is my aunt. He is my uncle.

She is our **niece.**

night   Night is the time of day when it is dark. Night starts when the sun sets and ends when it rises.

Grover sleeps with his teddy bear every **night.**

nine Nine is a number. Nine is one more than eight.

The Count has **nine** candles on his piano.

nineteen Nineteen is a number. Nineteen is ten plus nine more.

Bert has ten Figgy Fizz bottle caps and nine Prune Crush bottle caps in his collection. He has **nineteen** bottle caps all together.

no No means not true or wrong. No also means you will not or cannot do something. No can also mean not any.

Is your name Goldilocks?

No!

Hey, Bert, do you want to play football?

No!

Do you have any bananas?

No. I have **no** bananas today.

noise Noise is sound that is not pleasing to hear.

He is making a loud **noise**!

RAT-A-TAT-TAT!

none None means not any.

There were three bats in my belfry. They all flew away. Now there are **none**.

noon   Noon is the middle of the day. At noon it is twelve o'clock.

It is **noon.** The twelve o'clock train is on time.

nose   Your nose is a part of your face. You use your nose to breathe and smell. Look up the word face.

Grover is smelling a flower with his **nose.**

I love flowers. They smell so nice.

nothing   Nothing means not anything.

As you can see, there is **nothing** in my hat.

not   Not means in no way.

I love stinkweed. Stinkweed does **not** smell nice. It smells terrible. That is why I love it.

now   Now means at this time.

Do you want to go out to play, Bert?

Not **now,** Ernie. I'll play later.

number   A number tells how many.

I have
two plates.

I have
two carrots.

I have
two kittens.

Each monster has
the same **number**
of things.

nurse   A nurse is someone who takes care
of people when they are sick.

Farley went to the school **nurse.**
He took Farley's temperature.

nut   A nut is a dry fruit or seed
that is covered by a hard shell.

Oscar,
here is my
favorite kind of
food that begins
with the letter
N—**nuts**!

And here is
my favorite kind
of garbage that
begins with the
letter N—
nutshells.

Walnut   Pecan   Almond

Cashew   Chestnut

Pistachio   Coconut

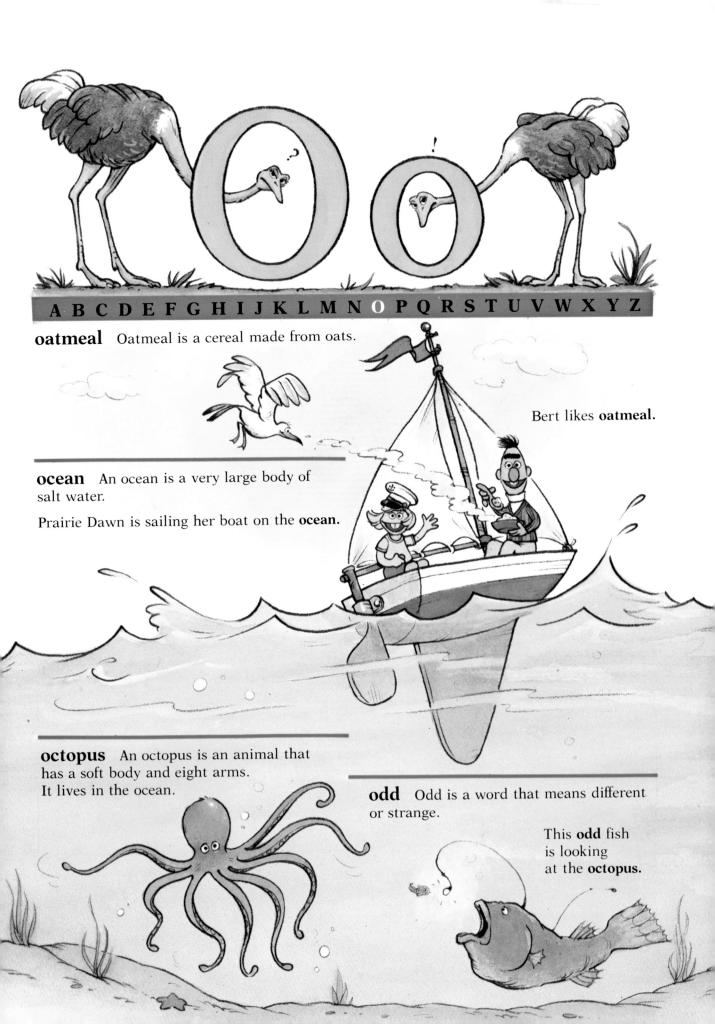

O o

A B C D E F G H I J K L M N **O** P Q R S T U V W X Y Z

oatmeal   Oatmeal is a cereal made from oats.

Bert likes **oatmeal.**

ocean   An ocean is a very large body of salt water.

Prairie Dawn is sailing her boat on the **ocean.**

octopus   An octopus is an animal that has a soft body and eight arms. It lives in the ocean.

odd   Odd is a word that means different or strange.

This **odd** fish is looking at the **octopus.**

of   Of means coming from or belonging to.

Half **of** the pie is missing.

of   Of also means containing or made from.

I have a loaf **of** bread, a jar **of** peanut butter, and a bottle **of** milk for our picnic. What do you have, Ernie?

I have this sign, Bert.

KEEP OFF THE GRASS

off   Off means not on.

off   Off also means not in use.

Ernie, you can turn **off** the radio. The Pigeon News is over.

office   An office is a place where people work.

Farley's mother is president of the Tick Tock Clock Company. She is working in her **office.**

Mommy, do you know what time it is?

often   Often means again and again.

Herry Monster **often** breaks things.

I can't help it.

old When something is old, it is not new.

How do you like these **old** rags?

Old also means how long someone has lived. I am five years **old.**

on On means touching or covering.

Marshal Grover is **on** his horse, Fred.

on On also means not turned off.

Shhh, Ernie. I'm listening to the radio. The Pigeon News is **on.**

once Once means one time.

Woof!

How many times did Barkley bark?

He barked **once.**

one One is a number. When you count, you begin with the number one.

1 ... **one** Cookie Monster!

only Only means by itself or no more than.

There is **only** one Cookie Monster.

Thank goodness! This is my **only** cookie.

open Open means not closed.

The door is **open.**

---

open When you open something, you uncover, unfold, unlock, or remove a part of it.

Ernie had to **open** his door...so he could **open** his mailbox...so he could **open** his letter.

---

opposite Two things that are opposite are as different from each other as they can be.

Big is the **opposite** of little.

Little is the **opposite** of big.

> We are sitting **opposite** each other.

> **Opposite** also means on the other side of.

---

or Or means one but not the other.

---

orange An orange is a round fruit that grows on an orange tree.

> Farley, do you want a grapefruit or an **orange**?

> I want an **orange.**

> **Orange** is also the name of a color.

Look up the word color.

orchestra   An orchestra is a large group of musicians playing different kinds of musical instruments together.

The Amazing Mumford is leading the **orchestra.**

ostrich   The ostrich is the largest bird in the world. It cannot fly but can run very fast.

Hey, Big Bird, the dictionary says that the **ostrich** is the largest bird in the world.

Oh, yeah?

other   Other means not the same as the one being talked about.

There is only one meatball on this plate. I ordered two meatballs. Where is my **other** meatball?

Here is your **other** meatball, sir.

our   Our means belonging to us.

This is **our** bicycle. The bicycle is **ours.**

out When something is out, it is not in.

Betty Lou is in the cannon!

Betty Lou is **out** of the cannon!

outdoors When you are outdoors, you are not in a building.

Bert is indoors.

Ernie is **outdoors.**

outside Outside means not inside.

What are you doing **outside** your nest?

I'm painting the **outside** of my nest today.

oven An oven is a closed space where things can be baked. An oven can be part of a stove.

Cookie the baker bakes bread in an **oven.**

over Over means above.

The Amazing Mumford waves his magic wand **over** his hat.

over Over also means again.

The trick didn't work, Mumphie. Do it **over.**

over Over also means the other side up.

If you don't turn your hat **over**, Mumphie, nothing can come out.

over Over also means finished.

The Amazing Mumford's magic show is **over.**

own When you own something, or something is your own, it belongs to you.

I **own** two broken umbrellas. Aren't they wonderful?

There is only one great O word. Can you guess what it is?

OSCAR

P p

A B C D E F G H I J K L M N O **P** Q R S T U V W X Y Z

package A package is a bundle or a box with something inside. Sometimes a package is wrapped in paper and taped or tied with string.

Hey, Bert, here's a **package** for you!

Nifty, Ernie! My pigeon T-shirt finally came.

page A page is a piece of paper in a book, a magazine, or a newspaper.

Everything I've ever wanted to know about pigeons is in this book, Bert.

But, Ernie— the **pages** in that book have nothing on them.

That's right, Bert. That's all I want to know about pigeons— nothing! Hee hee hee.

paint Paint is used to color or protect things. Paint is wet when you put it on something, and then it dries.

Biff and Sully are using green **paint** on the wall.

pair A pair is two things that go together.

Bert has a **pair** of gloves, a **pair** of Argyle socks, and a **pair** of saddle shoes on the clothesline.

pajamas Pajamas are clothes to sleep in.

Prairie Dawn is ready for bed. She is wearing her **pajamas.**

YAWN!

pal A pal is a good friend.

palace A palace is a very large and fancy house.

Prince Charming lives in a **palace.**

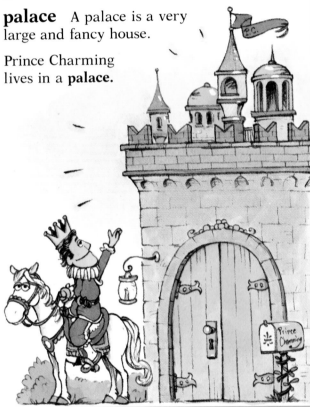

pan A pan is a metal or glass dish that is used for cooking.

Cookie Monster is frying an egg in a **pan.**

pants A pair of pants is clothing you wear over your hips and legs.

Bert cannot decide which pair of **pants** to wear.

paper Paper is flat and thin and is used to write and paint on. Paper is also used for wrapping packages and covering walls.

Three of these things belong together. One of these things is not the same.

The **paper** airplane, the news**paper,** and the magazine are made out of **paper.** The frying pan is made out of metal. The frying pan does not belong.

parade A parade is a group of people who are marching together—usually to music.

What is blue and red and purple and green and comes down the street making a lot of noise?

The Monster Day **parade**!

parent   A parent is a mother or a father.

I'm her mother.

I'm her father.

They are my **parents.**

park   A park is a place outdoors where people can have fun. Sometimes a park has a playground in it.

Bert likes to feed the pigeons in the **park.**

part   When you have a part of something, you have some but not all.

I have a whole apple.

Now I have **part** of an apple.

YUM!

party   A party is a group of people having fun together.

Hi, Oscar! I'm on my way to a birthday **party.**

Ugh! Birthday **parties** are no fun. Why don't you stay for my mud **party**?

pass   When you pass something, you go by it.

HOOPER'S STORE

We **pass** Mr. Hooper's store on our way to school.

paste   Paste is something you use to make things stick together.

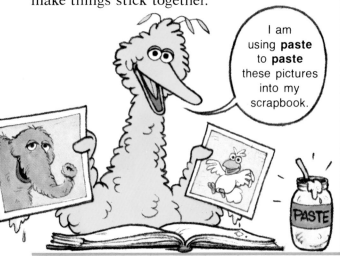

I am using **paste** to **paste** these pictures into my scrapbook.

pat   When you pat something, you touch it gently.

PAT THE DOG PLEASE!

patch   A patch is a piece of cloth or other material that is used to cover a tear or a hole.

There is a **patch** on Super Grover's cape.

path   A path is a narrow trail that people or animals walk on.

Little Red Riding Hood is walking on the **path** to grandmother's house.

GRANNY'S

pay   When you pay for something, you give money for it.

I will **pay** you fifty pennies for sweeping the floor.

Then I will **pay** you fifty pennies for a new bag of marbles.

MARBLES   MARBLES

MARBLES 50¢

MARBLES

pea A pea is a little, round green vegetable. Peas grow in pods on vines.

peach A peach is a round fruit with fuzzy skin and a pit in the middle. Peaches grow on peach trees.

peanut A peanut is a vegetable that grows under the ground. The seed inside the shell is good to eat.

pear A pear is a fruit with smooth skin. Pears grow on pear trees.

Big Bird is picking a **peach.**

Farmer Grover grows **peas** on his farm.

I can reach this **peach.**

I can reach that **pear** if I stand on this ladder.

I can reach this **peanut.**

pebble   A pebble is a small stone. A pebble is usually smooth and round.

peek   When you peek at something, you look quickly.

pen   A pen is a tool used for writing or drawing with ink.

pencil   A pencil is a tool used for writing or drawing. A pencil mark can be erased.

penny   A penny is a coin. A penny is worth one cent. Look up the word coin.

Each of the Busby twins has six cents.

people   Children, women, and men are people.

These are some of the **people** in Big Bird's neighborhood.

Plumber

Doctor

DOCTOR FRANKLIN

GROCERIES

Henry's BARBER SHOP

Carpenter

Barber

Garbage Collector

Grocer

Police Officer

BAKER

Baker

Mail Carrier

Fire Fighter

Paper Girl

Cab Driver

TAXI

TAXI

GAZETTE

MAIL

perfect   When something is perfect, it cannot be better.

Sam the robot makes mistakes. Sam is not **perfect**.

person   A person is a child, a woman, or a man.

pet   A pet is an animal that is loved by the person who takes care of it.

photograph   A photograph is a picture taken with a camera. The person who takes the picture is called a photographer.

The **photographer** is taking a **photograph** of Bert and his **pet**, Bernice.

piano   A piano is a musical instrument with white and black keys that you press with your fingers.

Don Music is playing the **piano.**

pick   When you pick something, you pull it away with your fingers.

Betty Lou likes to **pick** flowers.

pick   Pick also means choose.

picnic A picnic is a meal that is eaten outdoors.

I brought my favorite food to the Grouch Day **picnic**— sardines with chocolate sauce.

GROUCH DAY PICNIC

picture A picture shows how something looks. A picture can be a photograph, a painting, or a drawing.

This is a **picture** of me when I was a baby.

pie A pie is something to eat. Most pies are round and have a crust on the outside and a filling on the inside.

What does Frazzle Monster like to put in his **pies**?

His teeth!

GRUNT! GRUNT! SLURP!

piece A piece is one part of something.

I want a **piece** of pie.

pig A pig is an animal with four legs, a short nose called a snout, and a curly tail.

Farmer Grover is feeding his **pigs.**

I am a baby **pig.** I am called a **pig**let.

I am the **pig**let's mother. I am a sow.

I am the **pig**let's father. I am a boar.

pigeon A pigeon is a bird with a small head, a chubby body, and short legs.

Bert loves his **pigeon,** Bernice. Bernice loves Bert.

pile A pile is a group of things lying on top of each other.

Here is a **pile** of dirty laundry. I will wash it.

Here is a **pile** of clean laundry. I will fold it.

pillow A pillow is a bag filled with something soft. You can rest your head on a pillow.

pilot A pilot is someone who flies an airplane. A pilot is also someone who steers a ship.

place When you know where, you know the place.

pin A pin is a short, thin piece of metal used to fasten things together.

plain Something that is plain is not fancy or decorated.

plate 171

plan   When you plan, you decide what you are going to do before you do it.

I, Grover Knover, **plan** to ride my motorcycle up the ramp, over ten barrels, down the mountainside, and across the river and—

OOPS!

I did not **plan** to trip and fall.

plant   A plant is any living thing that is not an animal. Trees, flowers, and grass are kinds of plants.

plant   When you plant a seed, you put it in dirt.

Sam the robot is watering the **plants.**

If I **plant** this seed, it will grow.

Tomato Seeds

plate   A plate is a flat dish.

Monster dinners are really great! We eat the food— and then the **plate**!

play   When you play, you do something that is fun.

Big Bird likes to **play** hide-and-seek with Snuffle-upagus.

play   When you play a musical instrument, you make music.

Bert likes to **play** his accordion.

play   A play is a story that is acted on the stage.

The Sesame Street **Players** are performing a **play.**

please   Please is a friendly word to use when you ask someone to do something for you.

plenty   When you have all that you need, you have plenty.

plum A plum is a small, round fruit with smooth skin and a pit in the middle. Plums grow on plum trees.

These **plums** are ripe. They look yummy.

plumber A plumber is someone who knows how to fix the water and gas pipes in a building.

The **plumber** came to Farley's house to fix the kitchen sink.

plus Plus means added to.

Two **plus** one is three.

pocket A pocket is a place in your clothes where you can put things.

Prairie Dawn likes to keep her pet lizard in her **pocket.**

poem A poem is a special way of saying something. Many poems rhyme.

Mary had a little lamb. Its fleece was white as snow. And everywhere that Mary went, the lamb was sure to go.

point   A point is the sharp end of something.

The witch's hat has a **point.**

point   When something points, it shows the way.

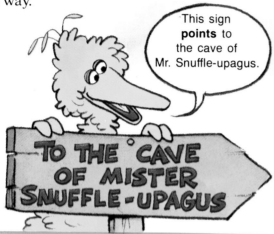

This sign **points** to the cave of Mr. Snuffle-upagus.

poison   Poison is something you should not eat or drink because it can make you sick or can kill you.

When I see one of these pictures on something, I know it means **poison,** and I should stay away.

pole   A pole is a long, narrow piece of wood or metal.

Oops!

Grover is painting the flag**pole.**

police officer   A police officer is a person whose job is to make sure people obey laws.

Mr. **Police Officer,** can you tell me how to get to Sesame Street?

Sure. Right after I give you a ticket for not stopping at that red light.

pond   A pond is a small body of water. A pond is bigger than a puddle and smaller than a lake.

Farmer Grover likes to swim in the **pond** with his ducks.

pony   A pony is a small horse.

Prairie Dawn likes to ride her **pony.**

pool A pool is a pond or a special place made for people to swim in.

Betty Lou likes to dive into the swimming **pool.**

poor Poor means not having enough money to buy the things you need.

I always send birdseed to my cousin Bartholomew because he is too **poor** to buy it for himself.

BIRD-SEED

poor Poor also means unlucky or unhappy.

Poor Bert. He is all out of oatmeal.

popcorn Popcorn is a special kind of corn that pops when it is heated.

The Count is popping **popcorn.**

... four hundred and ninety-three ... four hundred and ninety-four ... Oh, I love to count the pops!

porcupine A porcupine is a small animal covered with stiff, sharp hairs called quills.

I wonder why some people say that a **porcupine** is like a big pin cushion.

Oh!

PRESS

possible When something is possible, it can be done.

Is it **possible** that someone brave and smart and strong will hear us calling for help and come to our rescue?

It is **possible.** I can help them.

post office A post office is a place where people can buy stamps, mail letters and packages, and pick up their mail.

Marshal Grover went into the **post office** to mail a letter to his mother.

pot A pot is a deep, round container. Some pots are for cooking and some are for planting flowers in.

Oscar is growing stinkweed in a flower**pot.**

potato A potato is a vegetable that grows in the ground.

Farmer Grover is digging up a **potato** for his dinner.

Farmer Grover is baking the **potato** in the oven.

pour When you pour something, it flows from a container.

power Power is energy or strength to do something.

Pour me another glass of milk, Sam!

It gives me **power** to ride and rope.

practice When you practice, you do something over and over until you can do it better.

Big Bird is learning to use a lasso. He needs to **practice** more.

present A present is something nice you give to someone for a special reason.

pretend When you pretend, you make believe or imagine.

pretty When something is pretty, it is pleasing to look at.

price The price of something is how much it costs.

Pamela Monster is trying on a **pretty** hat.

prince A prince is the son of a king and a queen.

princess A princess is the daughter of a king and a queen.

prize A prize is a reward for winning or doing something.

Cookie the baker won a **prize** for the best cookie.

problem A problem is something that is difficult to do or a question that is hard to answer.

Biff has a **problem.**

promise   When you promise to do something, you agree to do it.

I **promise** to take good care of your plants while you are away.

protect   When you protect someone, you keep danger away.

Don't worry! I will **protect** you.

proud   When you feel proud, you feel good about yourself.

When I help people, I feel **proud.**

pudding   Pudding is a soft cooked food. It is usually sweet and is eaten as a dessert.

Mr. Smith wants **pudding** for dessert.

I'll have rice **pudding** ...

No, I'll have bread **pudding** ...

No, I'll have chocolate **pudding** ...

No, I'll have tapioca **pudding** ...

puddle   A puddle is a small pool of water on the ground.

Big Bird likes to step in **puddles** when he is wearing his boots.

pull   When you pull something, you take hold of it and move it toward you.

Farmer Grover is trying to **pull** his mule into the barn.

push   When you push something, you make it move away from you.

Betty Lou is trying to **push** Farmer Grover's mule into the barn.

puppet   A puppet is a doll that moves when you pull its strings or put it on your hand.

I want you to meet my **puppets,** Crummy and Yucchy.

put   When you put a thing somewhere, you place it there.

Mr. Chatterly is going to **put** his chair next to the fireplace.

puzzle   A puzzle is a toy with pieces that fit together.

This is my favorite **puzzle.**

puppy   A puppy is a young dog.

The **puppy** is following its mother.

It's no picnic being in this dictionary! I have to put up with all those dumb words like party, play, please, present, and pretty. I can't stand it!

Q q

A B C D E F G H I J K L M N O P **Q** R S T U V W X Y Z

quarter　A quarter is a coin. A quarter is worth twenty-five cents. Look up the word coin.

Each of the Busby twins has twenty-five cents.

I have a **quarter.**

I have twenty-five pennies.

quarter　A quarter is one of four equal parts of something.

Zounds! A **quarter** of the pie is missing!

queen　A queen is a woman who rules a country. A queen can also be the wife of a king.

The **queen** is sitting on her throne.

I proclaim today National Be Kind to Grouches Day!

Aaggh!

question　A question is what you ask when you want to know something.

Do you have any sardine ice cream with pickles?

The answer to that **question** is no.

quick　Quick means fast.

That brown fox is **quick.**

quiet　It is quiet when there is no noise.

At last it is **quiet** and I can get some sleep.

The Q section went quickly— but not quickly enough. I have just one question.

When are you going to turn the page so I can quit looking at you?

R r

A B C D E F G H I J K L M N O P Q **R** S T U V W X Y Z

rabbit   A rabbit is a furry animal with long ears.

race   A race is a contest to see who is the fastest.

The **rabbits** are about to have a **race.**

radio   A radio is a machine. When you turn on a radio, you can hear music or voices.

Bert is listening to the Pigeon News on the **radio.**

railroad   A railroad is a track for trains. A track is made with long metal strips called rails.

Look up the word train.

The **railroad** workers are working on the **railroad.**

rain Rain is water that falls in drops from clouds.

rainbow A rainbow is a strip of colors that you sometimes see in the sky when it rains.

raincoat A raincoat is a coat that keeps you from getting wet when it rains.

rake A rake is a tool used to make the ground smooth or clear.

Big Bird is using a **rake** to **rake** away the leaves.

ranch A ranch is a place for raising animals.

Rodeo Rosie lives on a **ranch.**

raw Food that is raw is not cooked.

Rodeo Rosie gives her horse **raw** carrots to eat.

reach   When you reach, you stretch out a part of your body to take or touch something.

Cookie Monster can **reach** the cookie jar on the top shelf.

When are we going to **reach** the next restaurant?

Reach also means to arrive at a place.

FOOD FUEL 5 MI.

read   When you read, you understand the words you see.

I ...
can ...
read.

I can
read!

ready   If you are ready to do something, you have everything you need to do it.

Hey, Bert! Are you **ready** to go to the costume party?

I'm **ready.**

Bert is not a **real** pigeon.

Bernice is a **real** pigeon.

real   Real means true. A real thing is not make-believe.

really   Really means truly.

That's a **really** scary monster costume you are wearing.

This is not a costume. I **really** am a monster.

reason   When you know why something happens, you know the reason.

Give me a **reason** why I should believe you are a real witch.

Oh!

recipe   A recipe tells you how to make something to eat.

Hey, Bert. What are you doing?

I'm trying a new **recipe** for oatmeal ice cream.

COOKING WITH OATMEAL

record   A record is a round, flat piece of plastic that can be played on a record player to make music.

I love to listen to my **record** of Chris and the Alphabeats.

I was born to add...

rectangle   A rectangle is a shape with four sides and four square corners.

Three of these things belong together. One of these things is not the same.

Three of these shapes are **rectangles**.
A circle is not a **rectangle**.
The circle does not belong.

refrigerator   A refrigerator is a machine that keeps food cold.

Ernie, don't forget to close the door of the **refrigerator**.

MILK

relative   Your relatives are the people in your family.

These are pictures of some of my **relatives**.

UNCLE UNO

FATHER

MOTHER

COUSIN

remember   When you remember, you think of something that happened in the past.

I **remember** when my Uncle Uno gave me my first counting toy.

rent   When you rent something, you pay to use it. You do not own it.

When did you get the new bicycle, Betty Lou?

It's not mine, Farley. I just **rented** it for today.

repair   Repair means fix.

Prairie Dawn can **repair** a broken chair.

GLUE

rest   When you rest, you nap or stay quiet for a while.

Big Bird needs to **rest** every afternoon.

rest   The rest of something is everything that is left.

restaurant   A restaurant is a place where you can buy and eat a meal.

Grover the waiter works in a **restaurant.**

return   When you return, you come back after being away.
When you return something, you give it back.

rhinoceros   A rhinoceros is a big animal with thick skin and one or two horns on the top of its nose.

rhyme   Words that rhyme sound alike at the end.

> I have been trying to think of a word that **rhymes** with **rhinoceros,** but it's impposserous—
>
> I mean, impossible.

Hat!

... **rhymes** with bat!

Duckie!

... **rhymes** with yucchy!

ribbon   A ribbon is a narrow piece of cloth or paper.

Bert tied a **ribbon** around his present for Ernie.

rice   Rice is a kind of grain. Rice grows above the ground in shallow water. Some cereals are made from rice.

Betty Lou is picking **rice.**

rich   When you are rich, you have lots of money.

Gourmet OATMEAL IMPORTED "FOR THE DISCRIMINATING PALATE" JUMBO SIZE!

> If I were **rich,** I would buy the biggest box of oatmeal in the whole world.

riddle   A riddle is a question that is also a puzzle.

ride   When you ride, you sit or stand while something carries you along.

Here's a monster **riddle.**

How can four big monsters **ride** in one tiny car?

Two in front and two in back!

right   When something is right, it is correct. It is not wrong.

Grover, you had two big boxes, and I gave you two more. Now you have four big boxes. **Right?**

That's **right!**

right   Right is also a direction. It is the opposite of left.

This is my **right** hand.

This is my **right** foot.

Right away means at once or immediately.

ring   A ring is a circle.

Rodeo Rosie is in the center of the **ring.**

Ring around a Rosie ...

A **ring** that you wear is a circle that fits around your finger.

ring   When something rings, it makes the sound of a bell.

Three of these things belong together. One of these things is not the same.

A telephone, a cowbell, and a bicycle bell are things that **ring.** A banana does not **ring.** The banana does not belong.

river   A river is a large stream of water that flows into another river, a lake, or an ocean.
Prairie Dawn is paddling her canoe up the **river.**

road   A road is a man-made path between two places. It is wide enough for automobiles and trucks to ride on.

The Count is driving his bat car along the **road.**

robot   A robot is a machine that can follow orders to do certain kinds of work.

Sam the **robot** can do many things that people can do.

rock   A rock is a piece of stone. A rock is hard and comes out of the ground.

I found a nice **rock** for your collection, Bert.

rock   When you rock, you move back and forth or from side to side.

Farley likes to **rock** in a **rocking** chair.

rocket   A rocket is a machine that moves through the air or up into space. Sometimes rockets go to the moon or other planets.

The **rocket** is taking off.

rodeo   A rodeo is a show in which cowgirls and cowboys ride horses and rope steers.

Come and see the **rodeo**!

roll   When something rolls, it turns over and over as it moves along.

Betty Lou's ball started to **roll** down the hill, and Barkley chased it.

roof   A roof is the top covering for a building.

Biff is fixing the **roof.**

room   A room is space inside a building. A room is surrounded by walls.

This **room** belongs to my cat, Fatatatita.

FATATATITA

root   A root is the part of a plant that is under the ground. Plants take in food through their roots. Some roots can be eaten.

Carrot

Rose

rope   A rope is a strong, thick cord that can be used to tie things together.

Herry Monster forgot to untie the **rope**.

rough   Rough means not smooth.

This ground is very **rough** and bumpy.

round   Something round is shaped like a ball or a circle.

Three of these things belong together. One of these things is not the same.

Pigeon Lover's Guide

An orange, a ring, and a wheel are **round**.
A book is not **round**.
The book does not belong.

row   A row is a line of people or things.

There is a **row** of birds on Bert's clothesline.

row When you row, you move a boat by pulling oars through the water.

Herry likes to **row** his **row**boat.

rubber Rubber is something that stretches and is waterproof. Many things are made out of rubber.

rug A rug is a cover for the floor. A rug can cover the whole floor or a part of it.

Bert likes to vacuum the **rug.**

ruler A ruler is a tool with straight edges. It is used for measuring length. Look up the word length.

The carpenter is using a **ruler.**
She is measuring the length of a board.

run When you run, you move very quickly on your feet.

Marshal Grover can **run** fast. Fred can **run** faster.

AH-CHOO!

A B C D E F G H I J K L M N O P Q R **S** T U V W X Y Z

sad   When you are sad, you feel unhappy.

Big Bird is **sad.**
He did not
get a letter from
Snuffle-upagus.

SNIFF

BIG BIRD

safe   Safe means not in danger.

The little pig is **safe.**
The big bad wolf cannot
blow his house down.

sail   A sail is a piece of cloth
that catches the wind.

sailboat   A sailboat is a boat
with one or more sails.

Prairie Dawn's
sailboat has
one **sail.**

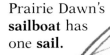

P.D.

salt   Salt is tiny white grains that come
from the ground or from sea water. Some
people put salt on food because they like
the way it tastes.

Sully is shaking **salt**
on his hard-boiled egg.

same When things are the same, they are like each other.

Cookie and Grover are wearing the **same** tie.

sand Sand is made of tiny grains of rock. You can find sand in the desert or at the beach.

Betty Lou likes to play in the **sand** at the beach.

sandwich A sandwich is two pieces of bread with some other food in between.

Here is my favorite **sandwich**— sardines and sour pickles on stinkweed bread!

save When you save something, you keep it in a safe place.

Bert **saves** bricks.

save Save also means to rescue someone or something from danger.

Uh-oh! There is someone who needs my help. I will **save** her.

HELP! HELP! Somebody **save** me from this furry blue monster!

saw A saw is a tool. It is made of metal and has teeth for cutting.

Prairie Dawn is cutting a board with a **saw**.

say Say means speak.

scale A scale is a machine that is used to weigh people or things.

Snuffle-upagus is standing on a **scale.** How much does he weigh?

scare Something that scares you is something that makes you afraid.

school A school is a place where you go to learn things from teachers.

scissors Scissors are a tool used for cutting. Scissors have two handles and two blades.

scream When you scream, you make a loud noise with your voice.

sea A sea is a very large body of salt water.

I like to swim in the **sea.**

Sea and ocean are two names for the same thing.

season A season is a time of the year.
There are four seasons: winter, spring, summer, and fall.

Farmer Grover works hard every **season.**

WINTER SPRING SUMMER FALL

seat A seat is something to sit on.

Three of these things belong together. One of these things is not the same.

The stool, the chair, and the bench are all kinds of **seats.** A cactus is not a good thing to sit on. The cactus does not belong.

second A second is a very small amount of time. There are sixty seconds in a minute.

The Count is counting the **seconds** on his bat clock.

One, two, three, four, five, six …

tick tock

second Second also means the one that comes right after the first.

Betty Lou is first in line. Barkley is **second.**

ICE CREAM

secret A secret is a special thing you know but do not tell.

I have a special hiding place, but you do not know where it is. It is my **secret.**

see When you look at something, you see it.

Whoops! Now you can **see** my **secret** hiding place. It is not a **secret** anymore.

seed A seed is the special part of a plant that can grow into a new plant.

Farmer Grover plants **seeds** in the spring.

selfish If you are selfish, you care about yourself and not about other people.

Cookie Monster! Don't be **selfish!** The cookies are for everyone.

COOKIES

sell When you sell something, you give it to someone and that person gives you money for it. After you sell something, it does not belong to you anymore.

I have to **sell** some of my old trash to make room for my new trash.

GARBAGE SALE

send When you send something, you start it on its way.

I will **send** a thank-you note to Granny Bird because she **sent** me some birdseed cookies.

set A set is a group of things that are alike in some way.

I have a **set** of blue dishes.

I have a **set** of yellow dishes.

seven Seven is a number. Seven is one more than six.

seventeen Seventeen is a number. Seventeen is ten plus seven more.

Bert has ten red bricks and **seven** gray bricks. He has **seventeen** bricks all together.

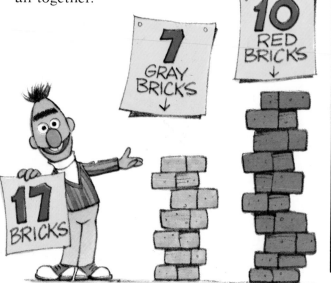

sew When you sew, you use a needle to pull thread through cloth or other material. You can sew by hand or by machine.

The Amazing Mumford has to **sew** a new button on his cape.

shadow A shadow is a dark shape. When a light shines on something, it makes a shadow on the other side.

Egad! Look at that **shadow** on the wall. I think someone is following me.

shake When you shake something, you move it quickly back and forth or up and down.

Ernie has to **shake** the dust out of the mop.

shallow Something that is shallow is not deep.

The water in this wading pool is too **shallow** for swimming.

Not if you are a little bird.

shape The form of something is its shape.

Here are some of my favorite **shapes.**

CIRCLE   SQUARE
RECTANGLE
DIAMOND   STAR

share When you share something, you let others use it or have part of it.

Here, Sully. I will **share** my sandwich with you if you will **share** that apple with me.

sharp Something that is sharp has a thin cutting edge or a point on the end.

Hey, you! Wanna buy this knife? It's so **sharp,** it will cut, peel, slice, chop, saw....

I don't want to buy a knife. But how much is all that wonderful garbage??

she She is another way to say woman or girl or female animal.

Prairie Dawn is busy. **She** is making a home for her pet spider.

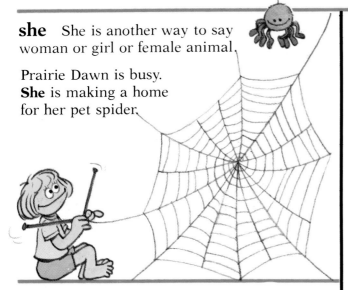

sheep A sheep is an animal that has four legs and is covered with wool.

I am a baby **sheep.** I am a lamb.

I am the lamb's mother. I am a ewe.

I am the lamb's father. I am a ram.

shell A shell is a hard covering. Some animals have shells. Some eggs have shells. Some seeds have shells.

Oscar, look at my collection of sea**shells.**

I have a **shell** collection, too, Betty Lou— egg**shells**!

shine When something shines, it makes a bright light. Something can also shine if light bounces off it.

Marshal Grover's badge **shines** because it is so clean.

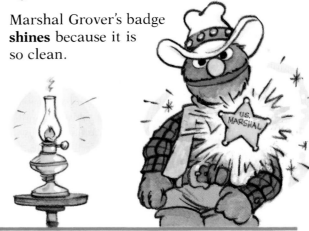

ship A ship is a large boat. Some ships have sails and some have engines. Some have both.

Captain Bert's **ship** is sailing into the harbor.

shirt   A shirt is a piece of clothing you wear on the top part of your body.

shoe   A shoe is something you wear on your foot.

Ernie is wearing a striped **shirt** and one saddle **shoe.**

shop   A shop is a store where you can buy things.

Cookie Monster loves to go **shopping** at the cookie **shop.**

short   Something that is short is not as high as something that is tall.

When something is short, the beginning is close to the end.

Big Bird is tall. Little Bird is **short.** Little Bird's jump rope is too **short** for Big Bird.

shoulder   Your shoulder is a part of your body. Your arms are attached to your shoulders. Look up the word body.

The Count's pet bat is sitting on his **shoulder.**

shout   When you shout, you call out loudly.

MUD! FRESH MUD! GET YOUR MUD HERE!

I love to hear the Mudman **shout.**

shovel   A shovel is a tool used to scoop things up.

Farmer Grover is using his snow **shovel** to **shovel** snow.

show When you show something, you put it where it can be seen.

show A show is something special to be seen or heard. A show can be a movie, a play, or a program on radio or television.

Grover Knover is putting on a **show.** Everyone is watching.

shut When you shut something, you close it.

sick When you are sick, you are not healthy.

Biff is **sick.** He has a cold.

side The side of something is the part that is not the top, bottom, front, or back.

Herry Monster is lifting a chest. There are two handles— one on each **side.**

sign A sign tells you something. A printed sign uses words or pictures. You can also make signs with your hands in special ways.

What do these **signs** tell you?

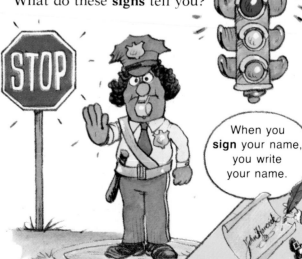

silent   Silent means without any sound.

Shhhhh! We must be **silent** while Mr. Snuffle-upagus takes his nap!

silly   When something is silly, it does not make sense and may be funny.

Fred, what happened to your head?

Isn't Marshal Grover **silly**?

sing   When you sing, you make music with your voice.

Bert likes to **sing** to Bernice. Bernice thinks he is a good **singer.**

Doin' the Pigeon...

single   Single is a word that means one.

I would like a **single** scoop of birdseed ice cream, please.

sink   A sink is a bowl that can be filled with water and has a drain to let the water out.

Cookie the baker has a **sink** full of dirty dishes.

sink   When something sinks, it goes down. In water, some things float and some things sink.

Grover's rowboat is beginning to **sink.**

sister   If your mother and father have another child who is a girl, she is your sister.

She is my **sister.**

He is my brother.

sit When you sit, you rest on the lower part of your body. Your weight is off your feet.

Why did the monster **sit** on the clock?

He wanted to be on time!

crunch!

six Six is a number. Six is one more than five.

sixteen Sixteen is a number. Sixteen is ten plus six more.

Oscar has ten red apple cores and **six** green apple cores. He has **sixteen** apple cores all together.

size The size of something is how big or how small it is.

Figgy Fizz comes in three different **sizes**— small, medium, and large.

skate A skate is something you wear on your foot to help you move on ice, hard floors, or sidewalks. Some skates have runners and some have wheels.

Betty Lou wears roller **skates** to **skate** on the sidewalk.

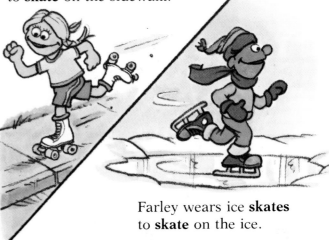

Farley wears ice **skates** to **skate** on the ice.

skeleton Your skeleton is all the bones of your body fitted together. All people and most animals have skeletons. Look up the word bone.

This is a picture of a human **skeleton.**

This is a picture of a dinosaur **skeleton.**

skin Your skin is the outer covering of your body. Animals and fruits and vegetables also have skins.

My pet snake, Sammy, has pretty stripes on his **skin.**

I do not have stripes on my **skin.**

skip   When you skip, you take little hops while you run.

I like to walk.

I like to **skip.**

When you **skip** something, you leave it out.

I read the whole dictionary and didn't **skip** one word.

---

skirt   A skirt is a piece of clothing. It hangs from your waist.

Rodeo Rosie is wearing a brown **skirt.**

sky   The sky is the covering of air and clouds over the world.

I love to fly my little airplane in the **sky.**

---

sled   A sled is something with runners that slides on the snow or the ice.

Betty Lou is coasting down the hill on her **sled.**

sleep   When you sleep, you close your eyes and rest your whole body.

Grover likes to **sleep** with his teddy bear.

slide   Slide means to move smoothly across a surface.

slide   A slide is a playground toy. After you climb to the top, you slide to the bottom.

Big Bird likes to **slide** down the **slide.**

slip   When you slip, you slide and start to fall.

slippery   Something that is slippery can make you slip.

oooOPS!

Banana peels are **slippery.** If you step on one, you may **slip.**

slow   Slow means not fast.

Barkley is watching a snail race. Snails are **slow.**

woof!

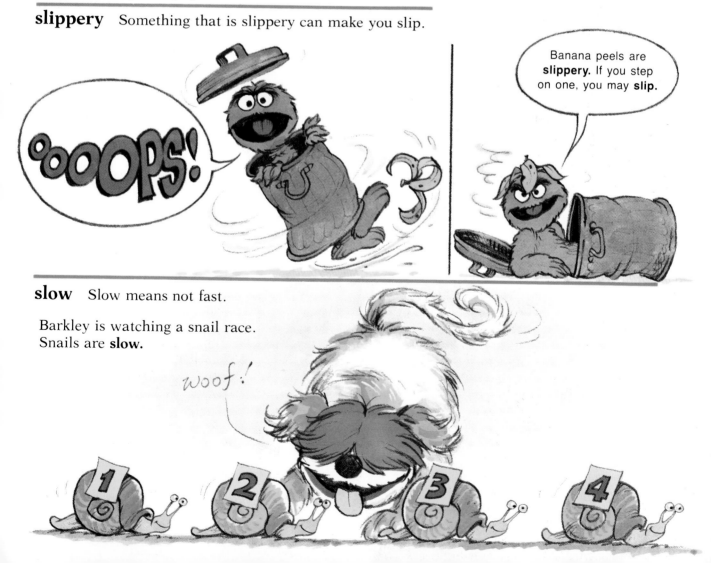

small Small means little.

Big Bird has a large mailbox.

Little Bird has a **small** mailbox.

smell When you smell something, you breathe an odor in through your nose.

Can you **smell** my stinkweek soup? Doesn't it have a lovely **smell**?

PHEW!

smile When you smile, the corners of your mouth turn up and you look happy.

Rubber Duckie makes Ernie **smile.**

smoke Smoke is the cloud that rises from something burning.

Prairie Dawn's campfire is still burning. She can see the **smoke.**

Where there's **smoke,** there's fire.

smooth Something that is smooth has a surface that is not rough or wrinkled or bumpy.

The sidewalk is **smooth.**

The road is bumpy.

sneeze When you sneeze, air comes out of your nose and mouth and you make a loud sound like AH-CHOO.

Pepper makes you ... ah ... AH ... AH ... CHOOOO! ... **sneeze.**

snow Snow is tiny white flakes of frozen water that fall from the clouds.

so So means very.

soap Soap is something used with water to clean things.

Ernie is cleaning Rubber Duckie with **soap.**

sock A sock is something made of cloth that you wear on your foot. You put on your sock before you put on your shoe.

There is a hole in the Count's **sock.**

soft When something is soft, it is not hard or stiff.

Three of these things belong together. One of these things is not the same.

A teddy bear, a pillow, and a blanket are all **soft** things. A lunchbox is a hard thing. The lunchbox does not belong.

son If a father and mother have a child who is a boy, that child is their son.

song A song is something to sing.

soon Soon is a word that means not too long from now.

sorry   When you are sorry, you are sad about something that has happened.

I'm **sorry** I broke your toy airplane, Farley. I'll try to fix it.

sound   A sound is something you hear.

Hey, Oscar! What was that terrible **sound** I heard a moment ago?

I didn't hear anything, Betty Lou. I was too busy playing my trombone.

soup   Soup is a liquid food made by cooking meat, vegetables, or fruits in water.

Hey, waiter! There's a fly in my **soup.**

Don't worry, sir. Flies don't eat much.

speak   When you speak, you talk.

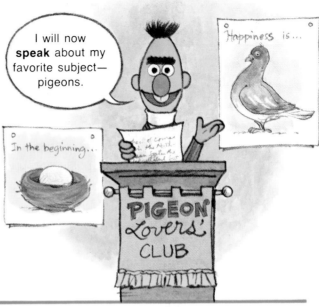

I will now **speak** about my favorite subject— pigeons.

Happiness is...

In the beginning...

PIGEON Lovers' CLUB

special   Special is a word that means not like all the others.

Mr. Snuffle-upagus is my **special** friend.

speed   The speed of something is how fast it goes.

Grover Knover can move with great **speed.**

spell When you spell a word, you say or write its letters in the right order.

Oscar can **spell** SCRAM.

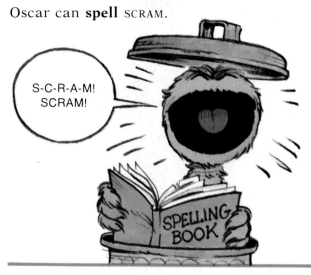

S-C-R-A-M! SCRAM!

spider A spider is a very small animal with eight legs. Many spiders spin webs to catch insects for food.

I am Miss Muffet. This is my pet **spider,** Stanley.

The SESAME STREET PLAYERS in Little Miss Muffet

spill When something spills, it falls out of a container—usually by mistake.

Farley did not want to **spill** his jellybeans. But he did.

spin When you spin something, you turn it around and around quickly.
When something spins, it turns around quickly.

Ernie likes to **spin** his top. His top is **spinning** fast.

spoon A spoon is a tool used to stir or scoop up food. You sometimes use a spoon when you eat.

Bert eats his oatmeal with a **spoon.**

spot A spot is a kind of mark.

Look! There is a **spot** on my cape. Let me count it. 1…one **spot**! Wonderful!

spread When you spread something, you smooth it out so that it covers more space.

Bert likes to **spread** peanut butter on a piece of bread.

PEANUT BUTTER

spring   Spring is the name of a season. Spring comes after winter.

The leaves on the trees are beginning to grow. It must be **spring.**

square   A square is a shape with four corners and four sides of the same length.

One of these shapes is not like the others. One of these shapes does not belong.

The circle does not have four corners and four sides. It is not a **square.** It does not belong.

squeeze   When you squeeze something, you press it.

Ernie has to **squeeze** the sponge to get the water out.

stage   A stage is the place in the theater where the actors act, the dancers dance, and the singers sing.

Big Bird is acting on the **stage.**

To fly or not to fly ...

stairs   Stairs are a set of steps. You can go up stairs and you can go down stairs.

These are the **stairs** to the castle tower. Let me count the steps. 1 ... one step ... 2 ... two steps ...

stamp   A stamp is a small piece of paper that you put on a letter or package to show that you have paid to send it.

stand   When you stand, you are on your feet, but your feet are not moving.

Farley has to **stand** in line to buy a **stamp** for his letter.

stamp

star A star is another sun—far, far away. At night a star looks like a tiny point of light in the sky.

Grover the astronaut can see many **stars.**

---

star A star is also a shape.

Grover's spaceship has a **star** on its side.

A **star** is also a famous person in a show.

clap clap clap HURRAY! clap YEA!

start When you start something, you begin it or get it going.

Grouches, **start** your grouchmobiles so I can **start** the race.

STARTER

START

stay When you stay, you do not leave.

Connie the witch is going on a trip. The other witches will **stay** at home.

steal When someone steals, that person takes something that does not belong to him or her.

Watch out for the Cookie Thief! He might **steal** your cookies.

WANTED The Great COOKIE THIEF

COOKIES

step A step is what you put your foot on when you go up or down stairs.

The stairs in my castle have five hundred and sixty-eight **steps.** I love to count them all. 1 …one **step** … 2 …two **steps** …

stick A stick is a long, thin piece of wood.

Barkley likes to play with a **stick.**

stick When you make something stick, it stays where you put it.

How do you like my latest work of art? I used glue to make all these pieces of garbage **stick** to my hat.

still Still means not moving or not talking.

Hold **still,** everybody!

ugh!

—ooch!

stone A stone is a rock. Some things are made out of stone.

Farmer Grover is lifting a heavy **stone.**

stop When something stops, it does not keep going.

Grover Knover has to **stop** at the **stop** sign.

store A store is a place where you can buy things.

Grover's mother bought a new book at the book**store.**

MR. SHAW'S BOOKSTORE

Goldilocks and the Three Bears

story A story is something to tell. Stories can be true or imaginary. You can tell a story out loud or write it.

stove A stove is a thing used for cooking or heating.

Grover's mother is reading the **story** of Goldilocks and the three bears.

Papa Bear was cooking porridge on the **stove**.

straight Straight means without a bend or a curve or a curl or a twist.

This is a **straight** line. The other lines are not **straight**.

straight line

crooked line

curly line

curved line

strange Strange means odd, unusual, or not seen or heard before.

There is a **strange** bird in Big Bird's nest.

A **stranger** is someone you don't know.

Hi. My name is Fred.

BUS STOP

street A street is a road in a town or a city. A street usually has buildings on it.

Sesame **Street** is a nice **street** to live on.

HOOPER'S STORE

SESAME STREET

123

TAXI

stretch When you stretch something, you make it longer or bigger.

Don't put my sweater on, Herry. You will **stretch** it.

string A string is a very thin rope.

Big Bird is tying a package with **string.**

strong Strong means having lots of power or not easily broken.

Herry can lift heavy barbells.
Herry is **strong.**

The third little pig's house was **strong.** The wolf could not blow it down.

subtract When you subtract, you take something away.

If I **subtract** one apple from four apples, I will have three apples.

subway A subway is an underground railroad. Some cities have subways.

Biff rides to work on the **subway.**

suddenly Suddenly means all at once.

The Monster Marching Band had to stop **suddenly.**

CRASH!

sugar Sugar is something you can put in food to make it taste sweeter.

This lemonade tastes too sweet. There is too much **sugar** in it.

summer Summer is the name of a season. Summer comes after spring.

sun The sun is a star. It gives light and warmth and energy to all living things on the earth.

The **sun** is the brightest light in the sky.

The days are getting longer and hotter. It must be **summer.**

super Super means extra-big, extra-strong, extra-smart, or extra-good.

I, **Super** Grover, am proud that I can help people with my **super** powers.

sure When you are sure about something, you know that it is true. You are certain.

surprise A surprise is something you do not know about or expect.

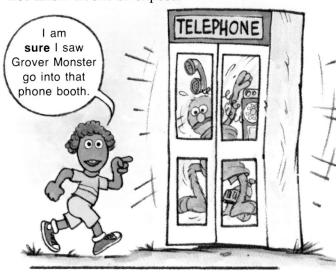

I am **sure** I saw Grover Monster go into that phone booth.

Super Grover! What a **surprise** to see you!

swallow When you swallow food or water, it goes down your throat to your stomach.

Sammy the snake will now **swallow** another apple.

sweep To sweep means to brush away. You can use a broom to sweep dirt.

This is the way I **sweep** my nest, **sweep** my nest, **sweep** my nest....

sweet When something is sweet, it is nice to taste or smell or hear or see. When something tastes sweet, it usually has sugar in it.

How **sweet!**

How **sweet!**

How **sweet!**

How **sweet!**

swim When you swim, you use your arms and legs to move through the water.

Prairie Dawn likes to **swim.** She is a good **swimmer.**

swing A swing is a hanging seat that moves back and forth.

What time is it when Herry Monster sits on your **swing**?

Time to get a new **swing.**

Just think of all the super words that begin with S— scummy, slimy, sloppy, soggy, stinky, swampy— and my special favorite— SCRAM!

Tt

A B C D E F G H I J K L M N O P Q R S **T** U V W X Y Z

table A table is a piece of furniture with a flat top and legs.

Lay your cards on the **table**, Rosie!

tail A tail is a part of an animal's body. Some animals have tails and some animals do not.

Different animals have different kinds of **tails.**

I'm an animal, but I don't have a **tail.**

take When you take something, you catch hold of it, or have it with you when you go somewhere. Take also means do or make.

Oh, Mommy, I am so scared of the dark.

Don't be frightened, Grover, dear. **Take** my hand and I will **take** you home. Then you can **take** your bath.

talk When you talk, you say words.

Biff likes to **talk.** Sully likes to listen.

Hey, Sully, what do you have in your lunchbox? I have a peanut butter sandwich. I love peanut butter....

tall Something tall is long from top to bottom. It is not short. The height of something is how tall it is.

I'm tall.

I'm taller.

I'm tallest.

taste When you taste something, you find out what flavor it has. You taste things with your tongue.

I can **taste** this lemon. It is sour.

I can **taste** this lollipop. It is sweet.

taxi A taxi is a special kind of car. You pay a taxi driver to drive you somewhere.

Bert and Ernie are going on a trip. They are taking a **taxi** to the airport.

teach When you teach, you help someone to learn.

teacher A teacher is someone who teaches—usually at a school.

Grover's **teacher** is trying to **teach** him how to write his name.

team A team is a group of people who work together to do the same thing.

My **team** is winning!

TUG of WAR CONTEST TODAY!

tear A tear is a tiny drop of water that comes from your eye when you cry.

Farley has **tears** in his eyes. He is crying because he dropped his apple in the sandbox.

tear When you tear something, you pull it apart.

I like to **tear** paper because **torn** paper is one of my favorite kinds of trash.

rrrrip!

telephone A telephone is used to send or receive sounds. When you use a telephone, you can talk to someone who is far away.

Big Bird is talking to Granny Bird on the **telephone.**

Gee, Granny. I sure like the birdseed cookies you sent to me.

I sure like the picture you sent to *me*, Big Bird.

television A television is a machine. When you turn on a television, you can see people and things and hear the sounds they make.

Bert is watching his favorite show on **television.**

tell When you tell something, you put it into words.

temperature The temperature of something is how hot or how cold it is. You use a thermometer to measure temperature.

Grover has a thermometer in his mouth. His mother is taking his **temperature.**

Don't feel bad, Grover, dear. I will **tell** you a story.

ten Ten is a number. Ten is one more than nine.

I have **ten** bats in my belfry.

thank   When you thank someone, you say you like what that person did for you.

Gee, Barkley, I want to **thank** you for finding my other shoe.

that   That means which or the one there.

LET'S MAKE A CHOICE!

Hi, folks! It's time to play— LET'S MAKE A CHOICE! Today's contestant is Betty Lou. Betty Lou, what's your choice— this or **that**?

I choose **that.**

THIS

THAT

Let's see what's inside the package **that** Betty Lou chose. It's ...

a year's supply of trash from Oscar the Grouch! Better luck next time, Betty Lou!

THAT

THIS

If you want to see Betty Lou play this game again, look up the words these, this, and those.

the   The means a certain one.

Bert, have you seen Rubber Duckie?

Do you mean **the** rubber duckie that I found in my paper clip collection, Ernie?

Bert's Paper Clip Collection

theater   A theater is a place where you can see a play or a movie or another kind of show.

The Count is arriving at the **theater.**

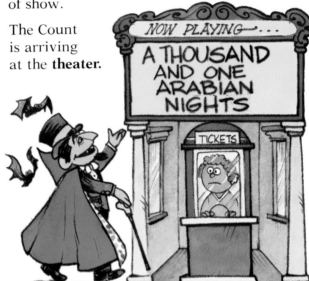

NOW PLAYING...

A THOUSAND AND ONE ARABIAN NIGHTS

TICKETS

their   Their is another way of saying belonging to them. When something is theirs, it belongs to them.

them   Them is another way of saying the ones I am talking about.

The Busbys are sitting on **their** bicycle.

This bicycle is mine. That bicycle is **theirs.** It belongs to **them.**

then Then means at that time.

A long time ago there was a little girl named Miss Muffet who was sitting on a tuffet eating her curds and whey.

Then what happened?

Well, along came a spider who sat down beside her.

Then what happened?

Little Miss Muffet shared her curds and whey with the spider.

there There means in that place.

Where shall I put this mud, Oscar?

Over **there,** in my mud box.

MUDMAN DELIVERY

OSCAR'S MUDBOX

these These means the ones here.

they They means the people or things I am talking about.

LET'S MAKE A CHOICE!

Well, Betty Lou, are you ready to play LET'S MAKE A CHOICE? Here is today's choice.... What do you choose, Betty Lou— **these** or those?

I choose **these.**

Then let's see what's inside **these** packages. Betty Lou, you chose . . .

a year's supply of sardine-and-sour-pickle sandwiches from Oscar the Grouch!

I don't like sardine-and-sour-pickle sandwiches. **They** make me sick.

THOSE

THESE

THESE

thick   When something solid is thick, it is big from side to side. When something liquid is thick, it is gooey and hard to pour.

thin   When something is thin, it is not thick.

thing   A thing can be seen or heard or touched or smelled. A thing can also be done or said or thought of.

Hand me that **thick** board, Sully. This board is too **thin.**

This paint is too **thick.**

This paint is too **thin.**

By the way, what is this **thing** we're building?

think   When you think, you use your mind.

Hey, Bert. Does this beach umbrella make you **think** of building sand castles?

No, Ernie. It makes me **think** of vacuuming the rug. That beach umbrella was full of sand before you opened it.

thirsty   When you are thirsty, you want something to drink.

Marshal Grover and Fred are **thirsty.**

Here you are— two big glasses of milk!

thirteen   Thirteen is a number. Thirteen is ten plus three more.

Bert has three big boxes of oatmeal and ten small boxes of oatmeal. He has **thirteen** boxes of oatmeal all together.

this   This means the one here.

those   Those means the ones there.

> LET'S MAKE A CHOICE!

> Here's our contestant, Betty Lou, back to play— LET'S MAKE A CHOICE! Once more, Betty Lou . . . what do you choose— **this** or that or these or **those**?

> **This** or that? These or **those**? **Those** or these? **This** or that? AARRRGGGHH! I can't stand it. Nothing! I choose nothing!

> Then let's see what you did not choose. In **this** package we find— a little puppy! In that package we find—a large bag of jellybeans! In these packages we find— cute, adorable kittens! And in **those** packages—a year's supply of coconut cream pies! I'm sorry, Betty Lou. And thanks for being such a wonderful contestant.

> If you want to see what Betty Lou is thinking, look up the word thought.

thought   A thought is an idea. A thought is what someone thinks.

Betty Lou's **thought:**

thread   A thread is a thin piece of string used for sewing.

three   Three is a number. Three is one more than two.

Farley is sewing **three** buttons on his shirt with **thread**.

through Through means from one side to the other side or from one end to the other end of something.

Barkley can jump **through** a hoop.

> **Through** also means finished.

> Are you **through** with that dictionary? I need it.

throw When you throw something, you toss it through the air.

> When I **throw** the stick, Barkley runs after it.

thumb Your thumb is one of the fingers on your hand. Look up the word hand.

> Ernie, why do you have a string tied around your **thumb**?

> So I won't forget to buy more string.

thunder Thunder is the loud noise you sometimes hear when there is lightning. Look up the word lightning.

KA-BOOM!

> Ahh. One lovely bolt of lightning and one fabulous clap of **thunder**! Wonderful!

ticket A ticket is a piece of paper that allows you to do something. Sometimes you pay money for a ticket.

tickle When something tickles you, it touches you lightly and makes you laugh.

Big Bird is riding on the train. The conductor is taking his **ticket**.

> Feathers can **tickle**.

> Hee hee hee ho ho ho ha ha ha ha hoo hoo hoo

tie When you tie a string, rope, or ribbon, you put a knot or bow in it.

Ernie can **tie** his shoelaces.

> A **tie** is something you can wear around your neck.

tiger   A tiger is a big, wild orange cat with black stripes.

I've always wondered if a **tiger** is orange with black stripes, or black with orange stripes.

I don't think I'll wait to find out.

ROAR!

tight   When something is tight, it fits too closely. It is not loose.

My Uncle Charlie knitted this nice sweater for me. But he must not know how much I've grown. Look how **tight** it is.

time   Time is when something happens. Time is measured in seconds, minutes, hours, days, weeks, months, and years.

What **time** is it, Ernie?

It's six o'clock, Bert.

Oh, good! It's **time** for the Pigeon News.

If you have a good **time**, you enjoy yourself. If you have a good **time**, you enjoy yourself.

He said that two **times**.

tired   When you are tired, you need to rest.

YAWN! Oh, dear. I am **tired**. I think I will go home to take my nap.

to   To means in the direction of.

Betty Lou is throwing a ball **to** Barkley.

today   Today is the day it is now.

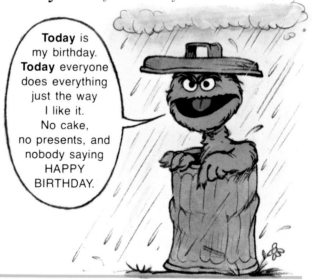

Today is my birthday. **Today** everyone does everything just the way I like it. No cake, no presents, and nobody saying HAPPY BIRTHDAY.

toe   Your toe is a part of your foot. You have five toes on each foot. Look up the word body.

Bert is doing his exercises. He is touching his **toes.**

together   Together means with each other.

tomato   A tomato is a round red fruit that grows on vines above the ground.

Tomato

Hi, Oscar! We are all here **together** because it's your birthday today.

Here is a cake made out of mud.

And here's a present from all of us.

Wow! It's a rotten **tomato**. It's just what I wanted. Gee, thanks, everyone, for such a perfect birthday.

Have a Rotten Birthday

tomorrow   Tomorrow is the day that comes after today.

I can't wait until **tomorrow**. Granny Bird just said she is coming to visit.

click

tongue   Your tongue is a part of your mouth. It helps you speak and taste.

Barkley likes to taste ice cream with his **tongue**.

tonight   Tonight is the night of the day that it is now.

Tonight I can see stars in the sky. That is the Big Dipper.

too   Too means also.

What is blue and furry and lovable and has eight wheels?

Grover on roller skates!

And I am *cute*, **too**.

too Too can also mean more than enough.

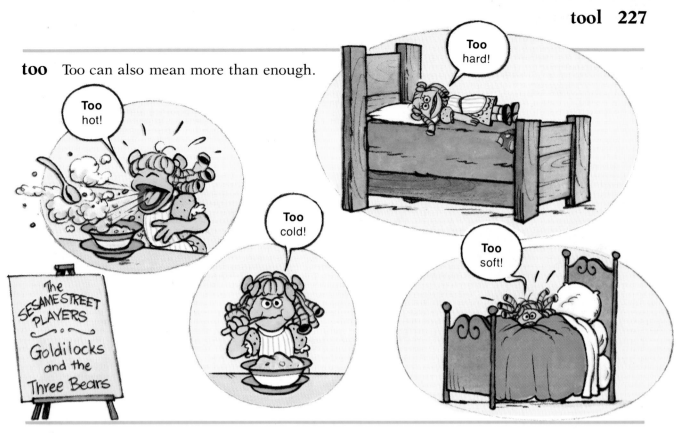

tool A tool is used to do work. Here are some different kinds of tools.

pencil
hammer
can opener
knife
hand drill
pliers
scissors
paper clip
screwdriver
wrench
spade
ax
saw
hedge clippers
sewing needle

tooth A tooth is one of your teeth. Teeth are in your mouth and are used for biting and chewing.

Frazzle is brushing his **teeth.** He has one **tooth**brush for each **tooth.**

top The top of something is its highest part.

Where did you put my ball, Bert?

It's on the **top** of the toy chest, Ernie.

A **top** is also a lid. My jar has a blue **top.**

touch When you touch something, you feel it with your hand or another part of your body.

I love to **touch** my little lamb. He feels so soft.

towel A towel is a piece of cloth or paper that is used for drying something wet.

Herry Monster took a shower. He is drying himself with a **towel.**

town A town is a place where many people live and work. A town is usually smaller than a city.

Marshal Grover is riding into **town.**

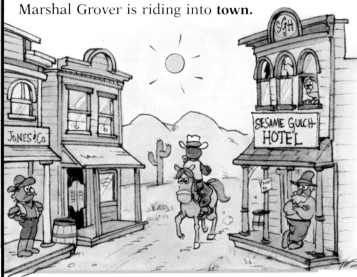

toy A toy is something to play with.

Three of these things belong together. One of these things is not the same.

Rubber Duckie, a toy airplane, and a jack-in-the box are all **toys.** Bert's shoe is something to wear. Bert's shoe does not belong.

train   A train is a string of railroad cars pulled along a track by an engine.

The cars have to stop so the **train** can go by.

trash   Trash is things that are thrown away.

travel   When you travel, you go from one place to another.

Whenever **I travel,** I collect **trash** on the way.

ROAD CLOSED

tree   A tree is a tall plant with a woody stem called a trunk. A tree has branches and leaves or needles.

Who is hiding behind each **tree**?

pine tree

palm tree

maple tree

triangle   A triangle is a shape with three sides and three corners.

Three of these things belong together.
One of these things is not the same.
The square has four sides and four corners.
The square does not belong.

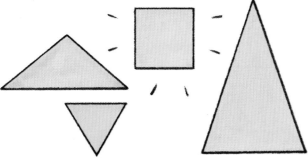

trick   A trick is a clever thing you can do.

The Amazing Mumford is doing a magic **trick.**

tricycle   A tricycle is something to ride. It has three wheels, a seat, handlebars, and pedals.

Barkley can ride a **tricycle.**

That is a good trick for a dog!

trip   When you go on a trip, you travel somewhere.

Farley is going on a **trip.**
He is taking the train.

Have a nice **trip,** Farley.

trip   When you trip, your foot bumps into something and you stumble or fall.

Grover, dear, be careful not to **trip** on the roller skate.

Oooops! You **tripped.**

trouble   When you are having trouble, you are having a problem.

Hey, Bert! I'm having **trouble** moving this box. What's in it?

Ernie, that's where I keep my rock collection.

truck   A truck is a machine with an engine and four or more wheels. It is used to carry loads or do other kinds of work.

I just love to count **trucks.**

true   When something is true, it is real. It is not false or a lie.

Is it **true** that a whale is the largest animal?

It's **true.**

trunk   A trunk is a big suitcase.

trunk   A trunk is also an elephant's nose.

trunk   A trunk can also be the woody stem of a tree.

I, the Amazing Mumford, will now pull from this perfectly empty **trunk** two other **trunks.**

A LA PEANUT BUTTER SANDWICHES!

1, 2, 3… three **trunks!** Amazing!

try   When you try to do something, you make an effort to do it.

I, Grover Knover, will **try** to jump over this pond.

Nice **try,** Grover Knover!

Try again.

turn   When something turns, it goes around and around or changes direction.

When I ride my bicycle, the wheels **turn** very fast.

When I **turn** a corner, I change direction.

turn   When one thing turns into another thing, it becomes something else.

When water freezes, it **turns** into ice.

ice cubes

water

turtle   A turtle is an animal with a hard shell and a soft body. A turtle can pull its head and arms and legs inside its shell.

Some people say that **turtles** can hide inside their shells and look just like rocks. Do you believe that?

Oh!

twelve   Twelve is a number. Twelve is ten plus two more.

Bert has ten blue shoelaces and two orange shoelaces. Bert has **twelve** shoelaces all together.

Twelve things make a dozen.

twenty   Twenty is a number. Twenty is ten plus ten more.

Ernie has ten red jellybeans and ten green jellybeans. Ernie has **twenty** jellybeans all together.

twin   A twin is one of two children who have the same mother and father and are born at the same time. Some twins look exactly alike. Some twins do not look like each other.

The Busby **twins** look alike.

The Henderson **twins** do not look alike.

two   Two is a number. Two is one more than one.

There are **two** Busby twins.

This dictionary is not as terrible as I thought. The T section has rotten tomatoes, garbage trucks, and trash, trash, trash!

Uu

A B C D E F G H I J K L M N O P Q R S T **U** V W X Y Z

ugly   When you think something is ugly, you do not like to look at it or hear it.

Oscar, please clean up this **ugly** pile of trash.

Ugly? I think it's beautiful.

umbrella   An umbrella is a folding cover that protects you from the rain or the sun.

When can three big monsters fit under a tiny **umbrella** and not get wet?

When it is not raining.

RRRR!

uncle   Your uncle is the brother of your mother or your father. Your aunt's husband is also your uncle.

Uncle Bob

Uncle Bob is my mother's brother. **Uncle** Lew is my father's brother.

Uncle Lew

Mother

Father

Me

under   Under means below.

Super Grover is flying **under** the bridge. Little Bird is flying over the bridge.

understand When you understand something, you know what it means.

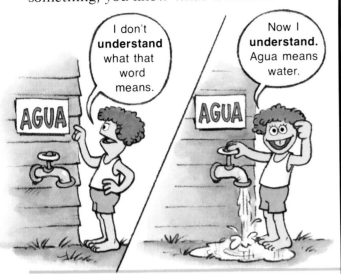

I don't **understand** what that word means.

Now I **understand.** Agua means water.

underwear The clothes you wear under your other clothes are called underwear. Undershirts and underpants are two kinds of underwear.

There are stars on the Amazing Mumford's **underwear.**

undress When you undress, you take off your clothes.

Ernie must **undress** before he can take a bath.

unhappy When you are unhappy, you do not feel happy—you feel sad.

Bert is **unhappy.** He lost his whole bottle cap collection.

until Until means up to the time of.

Farmer Grover always waits at the gate **until** the cows come home.

unusual Unusual means not usual. Something that is unusual is something that you are not used to seeing or hearing or feeling.

No, thank you.

Cookie Monster doesn't want any cookies. That is **unusual.**

up When you go up, you move to a higher place.

I am going **up** the ladder.

I am going down the ladder.

upside down When something is upside down, the top is on the bottom and the bottom is on the top.

Big Bird is **upside down.**

us Us is another way of saying you and me.

Look, Ernie! Here is a package for **us.**

Bert & Ernie
123 Sesame St.

use When you use a thing, you do something with it.

Hey, Bert. What does the word **use** mean?

Let's **use** the dictionary to find out.

usual Something that is usual is something that you are used to seeing, hearing, or feeling.

Bert is having his **usual** breakfast.

Bert, are you having oatmeal for breakfast *again?*

—YUM!

usually Usually means most often or in the ordinary way.

I **usually** complain at the end of each letter. So here I go. Where are all those other U words— like unbearable, unclean, unfriendly, unsightly, untidy, and unwelcome? This dictionary is unfair to us grouches!

V v

A B C D E F G H I J K L M N O P Q R S T U **V** W X Y Z

vacation   A vacation is a special time when someone does not work or go to school.

Guy Smiley is on **vacation.**

vacuum   When you vacuum, you use a vacuum cleaner to suck up dust and dirt.

Bert likes to **vacuum** the rug.

valentine   A valentine is a card that you send on Valentine's Day to someone you like.

Big Bird sent Snuffle-upagus a **valentine** on the fourteenth of February.

vase   A vase is a container used for holding flowers.

Mr. Snuffle-upagus sent me a flower for Valentine's Day.

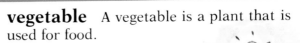

Big Bird put his flower in a **vase.**

vegetable   A vegetable is a plant that is used for food.

Farmer Grover is picking **vegetables** in his **vegetable** garden.

vehicle   A vehicle is something that can carry people or things from one place to another. Wagons, automobiles, trucks, and sleds are different kinds of vehicles.

I love to count **vehicles.**

very Very means more than usual or much.

My dog is big, but Barkley is **very** big.

village A village is a small town.

When the Count was born, his parents announced the news to all the people who lived in the **village.**

1... One Baby Count!

violin A violin is a musical instrument. It has four strings and is played with a bow. Look up the word bow.

The Count loves to play the **violin.**

visit When you visit, you go to see someone or something.

Prairie Dawn likes to **visit** the museum.

DON'T TOUCH!

voice Your voice is the sound you make while talking or shouting or singing.

Hello, Bird!

I can hear Mr. Snuffle-upagus' **voice.**

Vacation is a word that begins with V. I would be very glad to take a vacation from this dictionary.

Ww

A B C D E F G H I J K L M N O P Q R S T U V **W** X Y Z

wagon A wagon is used to carry things. A wagon has four wheels and is usually pulled.

wait When you wait, you stop what you are doing or stay where you are until something happens.

Fred has to **wait** for Farmer Grover to load the **wagon**.

YAWN!

waiter A waiter is a person who takes orders and serves food in a restaurant.

Waiter! What is this fly doing in my soup?

He is doing the backstroke, sir.

Grover the **waiter** is serving alphabet soup.

wake When you wake, you stop sleeping.

Wake up, Ernie! The Late Pigeon News is over. It's time to go to bed.

walk   When you walk, you move by taking steps.

Grover Knover's motorcycle is broken. He has to **walk.**

wall   A wall is the side of a building or a room. A wall can also be a kind of fence.

Biff and Sully are painting the **walls** of the room blue.

Oscar is building a **wall** around his trash can.

I **want** a **wall** around my trash can so people won't bother me.

want   When you want something, you would like to have it.

warm   When something is warm, it is more hot than cold. But it is not *very* hot.

The water in the bathtub is **warm**— just right for Rubber Duckie and me.

was   Ernie **was** dirty. Now he is clean.

wash   When you wash something, you clean it with water and sometimes soap.

Betty Lou likes to **wash** Barkley. Barkley does not like to be **washed.**

waste When you waste something, you do not make good use of it.

This oatmeal box is just what I need to make a drum. I'll just get rid of all this oatmeal . . . .

Don't **waste** that oatmeal! I'll use it to make oatmeal bread.

watch A watch is a small clock that you can wear on your wrist or carry in your pocket. A watch shows you what time it is.

Bert has a **watch** on his wrist.

watch When you watch something, you look at it.

Bert likes to **watch** the sun rise.

Today the sun is rising at six o'clock.

water Water is wet. We use water to drink, to cook with, and to clean with. All living things need water.

Herry Monster is taking a bath in hot **water.** He is drinking a glass of cold **water.**

way The way you do something is how you do it.

This is the **way** Ernie makes his bed.

This is the **way** Bert makes his bed.

way The way you go is the direction or path in which you move.

we We is another way of saying you and I.

We are going this **way.** They are going that **way.**

weak Something that is weak breaks easily or is not strong.

The toy wagon is **weak.** It will not hold Barkley.

wear When you wear something, you have it on your body.

Marshal Grover **wears** a hat, a vest, chaps, and a shiny badge.

weather Weather can be sunny, cloudy, rainy, windy, or snowy. The weather is also how hot or how cold it is outside.

The mail carrier has to deliver the mail in all kinds of **weather.**

Through rain or snow or sleet or hail, I see that Sesame Gulch gets the mail.

week A week is seven days long. Each day in the week has a special name. Look up the word calendar.

Bert has a busy **week.**

SUNDAY — Take Bernice for a walk.
MONDAY — Work on my bottle cap collection.
TUESDAY — Work on my paper clip collection.
WEDNESDAY — Buy oatmeal.
THURSDAY — Clean closet.
FRIDAY — Go to Pigeon Lovers' meeting.
SATURDAY — Polish saddle shoes.

weigh When you weigh something, you find out how heavy it is.

weight The weight of something is how heavy it is. Your weight is how heavy you are.

Stand still, Farley. I want to **weigh** you. This scale will tell me your **weight.**

well When you are well, you are not sick. You are healthy.

Farley is **well.**

You are very healthy, Farley.

When you do something **well,** you do it in a good way.

I roller skate **well.**

were The Busby twins **were** at the zoo.

We **were** both at the zoo yesterday.

You **were** there, too.

wet   When something is wet, it has water or another liquid on it. It is not dry.

Barkley is **wet.**

Now everyone is **wet.**

whale   A whale is a huge animal that lives in the ocean and looks like a fish. But it is not a fish. A whale breathes air.

The dictionary says that a **whale** looks like a fish but is not a fish.

AQUARIUM

what   What is a word used to ask questions or talk about people and things.

What are you holding behind your back?

I have **what** my mother gave me for lunch.

wheel   A wheel is something that is shaped like a circle and can roll or turn.

Three of these things belong together. One of these things is not the same.

The wagon, the tricycle, and the roller skates are all things that have **wheels.** The sled does not have **wheels.** The sled does not belong.

when   When is a word used to ask questions or talk about time.

When does Cookie Monster *not* want a cookie?

When he wants *two* cookies!

where Where is a word used to ask questions or talk about places.

which Which is a word used to ask questions or talk about people or things.

while While means during the time of.

whisper When you whisper, you say something very quietly.

Ernie has to **whisper** while the Pigeon News is on.

whistle A whistle is something that makes a loud, shrill sound when air is blown through it.

whistle When you whistle, you make a loud, shrill sound by blowing air through your lips in a special way.

who Who is a word used to ask questions or talk about people.

whole The whole of something is all the parts of it together.

whose   Whose is a word used to ask questions or talk about things that belong to people.

Egad! Footprints! **Whose** footprints are these?

I know **whose** footprints these are. Mine.

wide   How wide something is means how far it is from one side to the other. When something is wide, it is not narrow.

This doorway is not **wide** enough for me. It is too narrow.

wife   A wife is a woman who is married.

She is my **wife**.

He is my husband.

why   Why is a word used to ask or talk about the reason for something.

Why is there a WET PAINT sign on this bench?

WET PAINT

Oh! Now I know **why**.

WET PAINT

will   If you will do something, you are going to do it.

If you **will** say BLECCH very loudly, I **will** let you taste my ooky-gooky stew.

BLECCH!

win When you win a game or a race, you finish ahead of the others.

BIRD-SEED

COOKIES

FINISH

I **win**! Heh heh heh.

wind Wind is air that is moving.

The **wind** can make this toy pinwheel turn around.

The **wind** can make this flag wave.

Oops! The **wind** just blew my hat away.

window A window is an opening in a building or a vehicle to let in air or light. Most windows have glass in them.

Bert is looking out the **window.**

wing A wing is the part of birds, bats, and some insects that helps them fly. Airplanes also have wings.

My airplane has two **wings.**

All birds have two **wings.**

But some birds cannot fly.

winter   Winter is the name of a season. Winter comes after fall.

wish   A wish is something that you hope will come true. When you wish for something, you want it.

witch   A witch is a person with magical powers. Many fairy tales have witches in them.

Connie the **witch** is reading a story.

with   With means using or having. With also means in the company of.

woman   A woman is a grown-up girl. There is one **woman,** one girl, and one monster in the elevator.

wonder   When you wonder about something, you would like to know about it.

wonderful   Something wonderful is surprising or amazing. Sometimes the word wonderful is used to mean very good.

That's **wonderful**!

wood   Wood is the hard part of a tree. Many things are made of wood.

I like to build things with **wood.**

word   A word is a group of letters or sounds that has a meaning. You can say a word or read it.

There are so many **words** that begin with W. WOW!

work   When you work, you do something that uses energy. Most people work at jobs to earn money.

I **work** at the post office.

Special

I **work** at the grocery store.

I **work** at the hospital.

I **work** at the factory.

I **work** at school.

MATH

I am not **working.** I am resting.

world   A world is a planet. Our world is the planet earth.

I can see the whole **world** from my little spaceship.

worm   A worm is a tiny animal with a long, soft body and no legs. Earthworms live under the ground.

Slimey is my pet **worm.**

worry   When you worry, you are afraid that something bad is going to happen.

Be careful, Ernie! Those cups are going to fall.

You **worry** too much, Bert.

wrap   When you wrap something, you cover it.

I have to **wrap** this present for Mr. Snuffle-upagus.

write   When you write, you put words on something—usually paper.

writer   A writer is someone who writes stories, letters, or other things for people to read.

Herry is a **writer.** Does he **write** with his left hand or his right hand?

I **write** with a pencil.

wrong   When something is wrong, it is not correct. It is not true.

Farley has four apples. Right or **wrong**?

Wrong! I have only three apples.

I wonder where the words wart, weed, whimper, and whine went.

X x Y y Z z

A B C D E F G H I J K L M N O P Q R S T U V W **X Y Z**

x-ray   An x-ray is a picture of the inside of something. Sometimes the doctor takes an x-ray of your body to see if anything is wrong inside.

The doctor took an **x-ray** of Mr. Hooper's chest.

xylophone   A xylophone is a musical instrument with two rows of wooden bars that you hit with wooden hammers.

Frazzle likes to play the **xylophone.**

yard   A yard is a piece of ground next to a house or a school or another kind of building.

Biff and Sully are building a fence around their **yard.**

yawn   When you yawn, you open your mouth wide and take a deep breath. You yawn because you are tired or bored.

YAWN!

And I found this bottle cap on the sidewalk one day when I was walking home from the store. I had just bought some oatmeal . . . .

Bert's stories make Ernie **yawn.**

year A year is an amount of time that is three hundred and sixty-five days long. A new year begins with January and ends with December. Look up the word calendar.

Today is my birthday. Now I will have to wait a whole **year** for my next birthday.

yell When you yell, you cry out loudly.

Cookie Monster **yells** KOWABUNGA when he sees a pile of cookies.

KOWABUNGA!

yes Yes is a word you use to say that something is true. You can also use yes to say you will or can do something.

Cookie Monster, do you want a cookie?

YES!

yesterday Yesterday is the day that came before today.

Yesterday I washed the clothes.

Today I am ironing them.

you You means the person or persons spoken to.

This belongs to **you**, Ernie.

These belong to **you**, Bert.

young Someone who is young has lived a short time. A young person has not lived as long as someone who is old.

Farley is **young**, but his baby brother is **younger.** Their grandfather is old.

Farley

Grandfather

Baby Brother

your Your is another way of saying belonging to you.

yours When something belongs to you, it is yours.

Is this **your** umbrella, Little Bird?

Yes, that's mine. Is this **yours**?

yourself Yourself is sometimes used instead of you.

Mommy, I fell down.

Did you hurt **yourself**, Grover, dear?

Yo-Yo™ A Yo-Yo is a toy that goes up and down on a string.

Betty Lou is trying to win the **Yo-Yo** contest.

zebra A zebra is a white animal with black stripes. A zebra has four legs, a mane, and a tail.

Zebras look like striped horses.

And most of us live in Africa.

zipper A zipper is something that is used to fasten clothes or other things.

Ernie, please help me **zip** the **zipper** on my jacket.

Sure, Bert. But first I have to un**zip** the **zipper** on my sleeping bag.

ZIP!

ZOO   A zoo is a place where animals are kept so that people can see them.

Big Bird likes to visit the animals at the **zoo.**

HURRAY! There are no more words left in this yucchy dictionary!

But now I don't have anything else to complain about.

I think I'll go back to A and start over again.

Aa Bb Cc

Dd Ee

Ff Gg Hh

Ii Jj Kk

Ll Mm